A PEEK AT JAPAN

A LIGHTHEARTED LOOK AT JAPAN'S LANGUAGE AND CULTURE

FLORENCE E. METCALF

ILLUSTRATED BY "TOMOKO"

METCO PUBLISHING
Bellevue, WA

Copyright © 1992

by Florence E. Metcalf
METCO PUBLISHING
15805 S.E. 12th Place
Bellevue, Washington 98008

First Printing,   May   1990
New and Expanded Edition January 1992

The reproduction of any part of this book for an entire school or school system or for commercial use is strictly prohibited.

The purchase of this book entitles the individual teacher to reproduce for use in the classroom.

No form of this work may be reproduced or transmitted or recorded without written permission from the publisher.

Printed in the United States of America

Library of Congress Catalog Card Number 91-68043

ISBN 0-9631684-3-6

A PEEK AT JAPAN

Take a "peek"! What is really Japanese?

Japanese seldom wear kimonos . . . most Japanese still sleep on the floor . . Japanese writing is from top to bottom, and right to left . . . Junior High and High School students wear uniforms (earrings and curly hair are not permitted!) . . . rice is washed six or seven times before cooking, and eaten two or three times a day!

This book was originally written for American children, but adults have found it very informative . . . a little peek at Japan! Learn a few of the customs before visiting Japan . . . then maybe you won't put soap in the bathtub, and you will know what should always be said before eating anything! It's really very simple to count in **NIHONGO**! Learn to write and say your telephone number in another language! This book includes many glimpses into everyday Japanese life . . . expressions, customs, stories, festivals, songs, recipes, etc. A delicacy of the Orient is sensed in the artwork, sketched by my dear friend, **"Tomoko"**.

I express gratitude to my many friends, both American and Japanese, who gave me assistance and encouragement.

A natural empathy developed for friends and playmates during my childhood years in Japan. My hope is that the reader will better appreciate and understand the LAND OF THE RISING SUN and its people.

> Florence E. Metcalf
> Bellevue, Washington
> 1992

This book is dedicated to three young Bellevue students, RYAN, ERIC, and JEFF. They took a "peek" and wanted to see more, and more.

CONTENTS

Chapter 1   **EVERYDAY EXPRESSIONS**   1 – 12

Good morning, hello, good evening, thank you, you're welcome, good-bye, sleep tight. How are you? Fine. Please. I'm sorry. Expressions always used before leaving home and on returning home. Expressions always used before and after eating. I, you. What's your name? Yes, No. Photos – Children 7–5–3 Day.

Chapter 2   **COUNTING IN JAPANESE**   13 – 20

Numbers. How old are you? Months of the year, birthdays, telling time, telephone numbers. Where were you born?

Chapter 3   **WRITING NUMBERS IN JAPANESE**   21 – 28

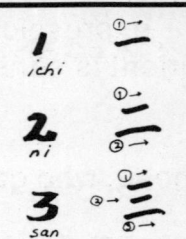

Learn to write 1 – 999, practice page. Follow-the-dots: crane, tea set, **TORII**, temple, **DAIBUTSU**. Mt. **FUJI**.

Chapter 4   **KANJI . . . HOW THEY DEVELOPED**   29 – 42

How they developed. Tree **KANJI**. **KANJI** game. Days of the week, months of the year. Three difficult **KANJI**: fish, horse, bird + crow. **KANJI** story.

Chapter 5   **SIMPLE PHRASES**   43 – 52

It is. Is it? Who, what, where, when, why. **KAO** face. Weather. Today, tomorrow and yesterday. Seasons. Very. Like, dislike. Colors.

| Chapter 6 | **FOUR WAYS OF WRITING** | 53 – 66 |

ROMAJI, HIRAGANA, KATAKANA, KANJI. Charts and examples. **HIRAGANA** face. **MOMOTARŌ** in English, **HIRAGANA** and **ROMAJI**. Photos – Teenagers and the Fan Dance.

| Chapter 7 | **THE JAPANESE HOMELIFE** | 67 – 82 |

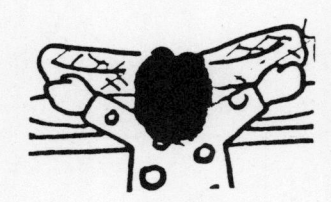

Home, **KŌTATSU**, bedroom, living room + bedroom, bath room + bath, kitchen. Japanese food – breakfast, lunch, dinner, rice cooking. Recipe – **OYAKO DONBURI, SUSHI.** Family, school and uniforms. Photo – **HARU'S SEIJINSHIKI.**

| Chapter 8 | **FESTIVALS AND FUN THINGS** | 83 – 96 |

New Years' Festival, **SETSUBUN, DARUMA,** Girl's Day, Boy's Day, **TANABATA, BON ODORI, JŪGOYA,** tooth fairy, **KENDAMA,** 7-5-3 day, a wedding picture, No. 4, **IKEBANA.**

| Chapter 9 | **STORIES, SONGS, ORIGAMI, KAO** | 97 – 118 |

STORIES: **MOMOTARŌ,** The Fairy Crane, The Tongue-cut Sparrow. SONGS: Rain song, Pigeon Song, Setting Sun, Hare and Tortoise, Tulip Song, **SAKURA,** Finger Game, Tongue twister. ORIGAMI: bird, helmet, balloon, box, crane. Photos – Tokyo and Japanese food.

| Chapter 10 | **THIS AND THAT** | 119 – 136 |

Japanese money. How much? Cheap, expensive. Letters and stamps. Animal talk! **JANKENPON.** Three famous monkeys! **MOSHI-MOSHI, NEKO YANAGI, HASHI** and **HASHI OKI,** map of Japan. The Emperor and Empress, the Japanese flag. **KANJI** for **KAO.OWARI** (the end!)

Throughout this book you will notice that most letters in the Japanese words are pronounced differently than they sound to us! The chart below may help you remember that . . .

                             is like the

Japanese sound	English sound	in
a	ah	amen
i	ee	easy
u	oo	zoo
e	eh	test
o	o	open
ai	i	tie
ii	ee	even
ei	ay	pay
oi	oy	toy

* If there is a bar over the Japanese word, it means you should hold the sound a little longer. Number 10 is JŪ pronounced joooo! (like oooo in zoo)

* The *"r"* sound is more like a *"d"* sound to Western ears! It is almost a cross between an *"r"* and a *"d"*. Sometimes it may sound a little like an *"l"*, too! This is a strange sound to us! THANK YOU is **ARIGATO** (p. 3). When you say this, twist your tongue to combine *"l"*, *"d"* and *"r"*! Impossible, you say! When I say *"ALIGATO"* to my Japanese friends — they say, "Perfect pronunciation". Then I say *"ADIGATO"* and they say, "Isn't that what you just said?" Sometimes foreign ears hear differently! We spell "Thank you", ARIGATO!! Confusing isn't it?

* The printed *"m"* often sounds like an *"n"*. Most Americans know what **TEMPURA** is, but it should be pronounced . . . TENPURA!

Remember these few rules and you will surprise your Japanese friends with your good pronunciation! They will say "**JŌZU DESU**" or "You speak very well!"

Chapter 1

EVERYDAY EXPRESSIONS

"Good morning."   "Hello."   "Good evening."

"Thank you."   "You're welcome."

"Goodbye."   "Good night."

"How are you?"   "Fine, thank you."

"Please."

"I'm sorry."   "Excuse me." (to get someone's attention)

Before and after meals . . . . . (always say this.)

When leaving home, and returning home . . . (always say this)

I – you. Mine – yours

Name. What is your name? Yes, No.

Photos – 7-5-3 Day.

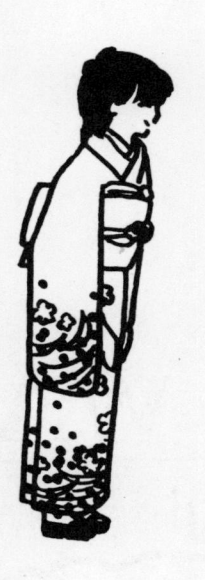

MAI NICHI

毎日の会話

EVERYDAY EXPRESSIONS

(oh–hah–yoh
OHAYO
goh–zah–ee–mahss)
GOZAIMASU
Good morning!

(kohn–nee–chee wah)
KONNICHI WA
Good Day!

(kohn–bahn wah)
KONBAN WA
Good evening!

2

THANK YOU – YOU'RE WELCOME

(ah–ree–gah–toh)
ARIGATŌ
Thank you

(dōh–moh)
DŌMO
ARIGATŌ
Thank you very much!

"DŌMO ARIGATŌ"

(dōh–ee–tah–shee   mah–sh–teh)
DOITASHI MASHITE
You're welcome!

"DŌMO ARIGATŌ"

"DOITASHI-MASHITE"

"IT SOUNDS A LITTLE LIKE "DON'T TOUCH MY MOUSTACHE!!""

3

GOOD BYE — GOOD NIGHT

(sah–yōh–nah–rah)
SAYONARA
Good bye!

See you tomorrow! Bye!

Sayōnara

(oh–yah–soo–mee–nah–sahee)
OYASUMINASAI
Good night! Sleep well!

OYASUMINASAI OKĀSAN

OKĀSAN
"mother"

YASUMI
"to sleep"

4

HOW ARE YOU?
How are you?

(gehn kee   deh ss   kah)
GENKI DESU KA?

or

(oh–gehn kee   deh ss   kah)
OGENKI DESU KA?

"O" makes it polite. Only use this when speaking **to** or **about** another person.

Konnichi wa- Ogenki desuka? How are you?

Hai! Genki desu. I'm fine

(kohn–nee–chee   wah
KONNICHI WA
Hello! & Good Day

The word for DAY is NICHI

KON means THIS

(ee–kah–gah   dehss   kah)
IKAGA DESU KA?

is sometimes said instead of ## GENKI DESU KA?

5

KUDASAI – Please
(koo-dah-sah-ee)

(hahm-bāh-gāh)
HAMBĀGĀ KUDASAI

Would you like a hamburger or a hot dog?

(ah-ree-gah-tōh)
ARIGATŌ

(dōh-ee-tah-shee-mah-shee-teh)
DOITASHIMASHITE

(goh–mehn   nah–sah–ee)
GOMEN NASAI
I'm sorry!

"Gomen-nasai."

"It really was an accident, mother! I'm sorry!"

(go–mehn   koo–dah–sahee)
GOMEN KUDASAI
Excuse me!

Gomen Kudasai

Entering:
"Excuse me please — Is anyone at home?" *and when you are trying to attract someone's attention.*

AT MEALTIME

These daily expressions are very important!
(It is difficult to give an accurate translation)

(ee–tah   dah–kee   mahss)
ITADAKI MASU

I'll eat now

Itadaki masu.

Always say this before you eat anything!

(goh–chee–sōh–   sah–mah)
GOCHISŌ SAMA

(deshh – tah)
DESHITA

Gochisō sama deshita

It was good

Always say this before you leave the table!

8

DAILY EXPRESSION

When you leave home for school or play mother says...

(ee–teh   ee–rahsh–ah–ee)
ITTE – IRASSHAI
"Bye – see you soon"

and you reply...

(ee–teh   kee–mahssoo or mahss)
ITTE – KIMASU
"Bye – I'll be back!"

When you return you say...

(tah–dah   ee–mah)
TADAIMA
"I'm home!"

and mother says...
(or the person in the house)

(oh–kah–eh–ree   nah–sahee)
OKAERI NASAI
"Welcome – I'm home!"

EVERYDAY EXPRESSIONS

(wah–tah–shee)
WATASHI
I

(ah–nah–tah)
ANATA
you

WATASHI NO
mine

ANATA NO
yours

WATASHI NO HANA
my nose

ANATA NO KUCHI
your mouth

(nah–mah–eh)
NAMAE
name

(nah-mah-eh   wah   nahn   dehss   kah?)
NAMAE WA NAN DESU KA?
What is your name?

NAMAE WA RYAN DESU
My name is Ryan.

(hah–ee)
HAI – YES
(ee–eh)
IIE – NO

(Speech bubbles: "Namae wa Alice desu ka?" / "Iie, Betty desu.")

NAMAE WA ALICE   DESU KA?
Is your name   Alice?

IIE, BETTY DESU.
No, it's Betty.

(ah–nah–tah   no   nah–mah–eh   wah   nahn   dehss   kah)
ANATA NO NAMAE WA NAN DESU KA?
What is your name?

11

3-5-7 Day – SHICHI–GO–SAN FESTIVAL
November 15

Read about this special children's festival on p. 94.

RYŪSUKE is wearing a **HAKAMA** – a long pleated skirt – a carryover from ancient days.

CHIAKI and **CHIKA** are visiting the shrine. They are dressed in colorful **KIMINOS** with long sleeves, flowers in their hair – and pretty **ZORI** and **TABI** on their feet.

Lots of pictures are taken on this day for the family album. **RYŪSUKE**, **CHIAKI** and **CHIKA** went to nursery and elementary school in Bellevue, Washington.

Chapter 2

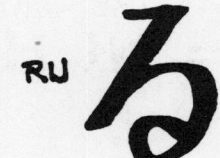

Count in Japanese

Counting 1 – 999

How old are you?

Months of the year . . . your birthday month.

Happy Birthday.

What time is it?

What is your telephone number?

Where were you born?

In Japanese
(nee–hohn–goh deh
<u>**NIHONGO DE**</u>
kah–zoh–eh–roo)
<u>**KAZOERU**</u>
Count

日本語で数える

NI
HON
GO
DE
KAZO
E
RU

COUNT IN JAPANESE

COUNT IN JAPANESE

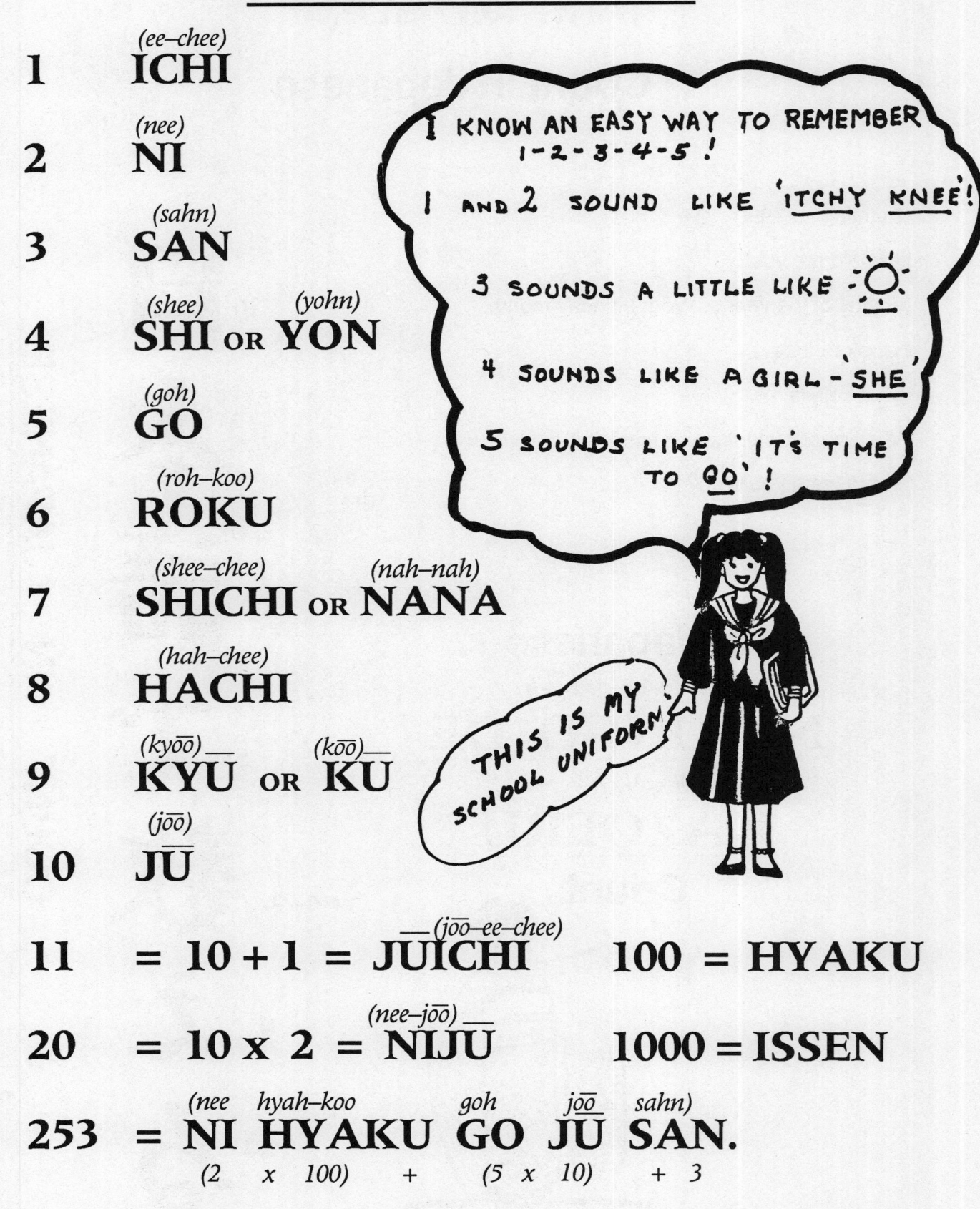

1 *(ee–chee)* **ICHI**

2 *(nee)* **NI**

3 *(sahn)* **SAN**

4 *(shee)* **SHI** or *(yohn)* **YON**

5 *(goh)* **GO**

6 *(roh–koo)* **ROKU**

7 *(shee–chee)* **SHICHI** or *(nah–nah)* **NANA**

8 *(hah–chee)* **HACHI**

9 *(kyōō)* **KYU** or *(kōō)* **KU**

10 *(jōō)* **JU**

> I KNOW AN EASY WAY TO REMEMBER 1-2-3-4-5!
>
> 1 AND 2 SOUND LIKE 'ITCHY KNEE'!
>
> 3 SOUNDS A LITTLE LIKE ☀
>
> 4 SOUNDS LIKE A GIRL - 'SHE'
>
> 5 SOUNDS LIKE 'IT'S TIME TO GO'!

> THIS IS MY SCHOOL UNIFORM

11 = 10 + 1 = *(jōō–ee–chee)* **JUICHI**   100 = **HYAKU**

20 = 10 × 2 = *(nee–jōō)* **NIJU**   1000 = **ISSEN**

253 = *(nee hyah–koo goh jōō sahn)* **NI HYAKU GO JU SAN.**
       (2 × 100) + (5 × 10) + 3

HOW OLD ARE YOU?

(nahn–sahee   deh–ss   kah)
NANSAI DESU KA?
OR   *(ee–koo–tsoo   dehss   kah)*
IKUTSU DESU KA

Now I know all my numbers. All I have to do is add SAI

1   **ISSAI**   *(ees–sah–ee)*
2   **NISAI**   *(nee–sah–ee)*
3   **SANSAI**   *(sahn–sah–ee)*
4   **YONSAI**   *(yohn–sah–ee)*
   never SHI SAI!
5   **GOSAI**   *(goh–sah–ee)*
6   **ROKUSAI**   *(roh–koo–sah–ee)*
7   **NANASAI**   *(nah–nah–sah–ee)*
   not SHICHI SAI!
8   **HASSAI**   *(hahs–sah–ee)*
9   **KYŪSAI**   *(kyoo–sah–ee)*
   not KŪSAI!
10   **JŪSAI**   *(joo–sah–ee)*
40   **YONJŪ SAI**   *(yohn–joo–sah–ee)*
   4 x 10
14   **JŪYON SAI**   *(joo–yohn–sah–ee)*
   10 + 4

HASSAI DESU

I'm eight years old.
How old are you?

15

MONTH = GATSU
(gah–tsoo)

Moon and Month are the same KANJI
Can you tell me your Birthday Month?

That's easy! All I have to do is add GATSU to the MONTH number.

CAN YOU WRITE YOUR BIRTHDAY MONTH?

ICHI GATSU January
NI GATSU February
SAN GATSU March
SHI GATSU April
  (not YON GATSU)
GO GATSU May
ROKU GATSU June
SHICHI GATSU July
  (not NANA GATSU)
HACHI GATSU August
KŪ GATSU September
  (not KYU GATSU)
JŪ GATSU October
JŪ ICHI GATSU November
JŪ NI GATSU December

TANJŌBI
Birthday

(tahn–jōh–bee   o–meh–deh–tōh)
TANJŌBI OMEDETŌ
Happy Birthday!

OMEDETŌ means CONGRATULATIONS!

(nahn   sah–ee   deh–ss   kah)
NAN SAI DESU KA?
How old are you?

I'M TEN. JŪSSAI DESU

(nahn   gah–tsoo   oo–mah–reh   dehss   kah)
NAN GATSU UMARE DESU KA?
In which month were you born?

(sahn   gah–tsoo   oo–mah–reh   dehss)
SAN GATSU UMARE DESU
I was born in March.
In which month were you born?

JIKAN – TIME
(jee kahn)

(nahn)
NAN – what

(jee)
JI – time

(nahn jee dehss kah)
NANJI DESU KA
What time is it?

(hah-chee-jee dehss)
HACHIJI DESU
It's eight o'clock

It's eight o'clock

(mah-ee) **MAE** before

(soo-gee) **SUGI** past

(hahn) **HAN** ½ or 30 minutes

(poo-n) or *(foo-n)* **PUN** or **FUN** minute

5:30   GO JI HAN DESU   (five o'clock half it is)

8:13   HACHI JI JŪSAN PUN SUGI DESU
(eight o'clock thirteen minutes after it is)

8:57   KYŪJI SAN PUN MAI DESU.
(nine o'clock – three minutes – before – it is)

(dehn wah bahn goh)
DENWA BANGO
Telephone Number

(ah nah tah noh
ANATA NO
your

dehn wah
DENWA
telephone

bahn goh
BANGO
number

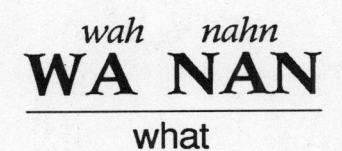

wah nahn   *dehss   kah)*
WA NAN   **DESU KA?**
what   is it?

dehn–wah   bahn – goh   wah   nee   sahn   goh
DENWA BANGO WA NI–SAN–GO
My telephone number is   2   3   5

roh – koo   zeh–roh   ee – chee   koō   dehss
ROKU – ZERO – ICHI – KŪ DESU
    6   0   1   9

What is your phone number?
*Say it in Japanese and write it
in two different ways. (Example: 2 could be "ni" or 二.)*

19

WHERE WERE YOU BORN?

UMARE – to be born

(ah nah tah   wah   doh koh
ANATA WA DOKO
you　　　　　　　where

oo mah reh   dehss   kah?)
UMARE DESU KA?
born

Where were you born?

VANCOUVER?
(bahn–coo–bah)

DALLAS?
(dah–rah–ss)

LOS ANGELES?
(roh–soo–ahn–jeh–roo–soo)

Remember:
the "oo" sound is like "oo" in zoo.

WATASHI WA
I

(shee–ah–toh–roo)
SHIATORU UMARE DESU
Seattle　　　　born　　　was

I was born in Seattle.
Where were you born?

20

Chapter 3

Write Numbers In Japanese

Numbers 1 – 999

Practice sheet

Follow-the-dot . . . "Crane"

Follow-the-dot . . . "Tea Set"

Follow-the-dot . . . "Miyajima Torii"

Follow-the-dot . . . Nara Temple and Kamakura Daibutsu

Follow-the-dot . . . Mt. FUJI

(soo–jee oh
SUJI WO

nee–hohn–goh deh
NIHONGO DE

kah–kee–mah-shōh)
KAKIMASHŌ

数字を日本語で書きましょう

SU JI WO NI HON GO DE KA KI MA SHŌ

numbers in Japanese let's write

Let's learn to write
NUMBERS
in Japanese.

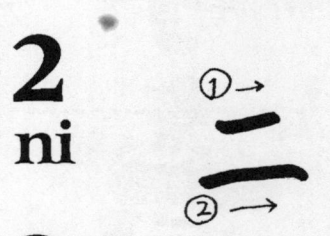

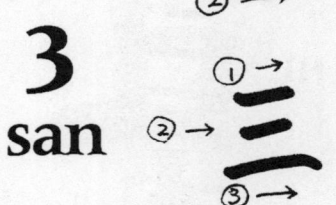

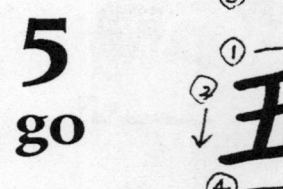

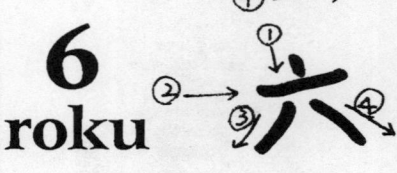

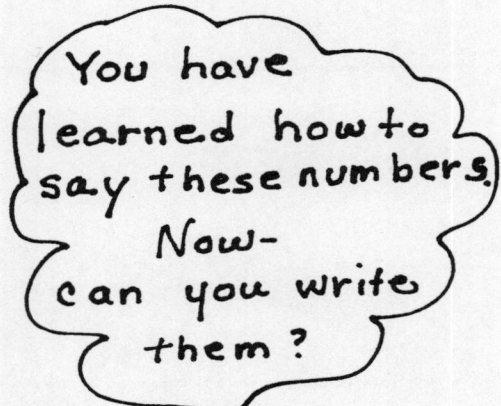

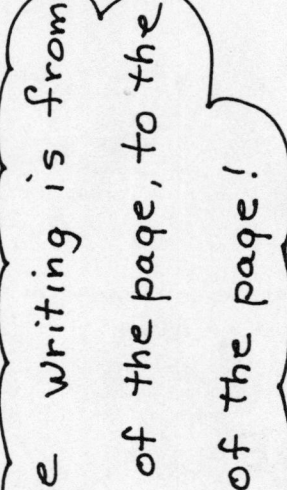

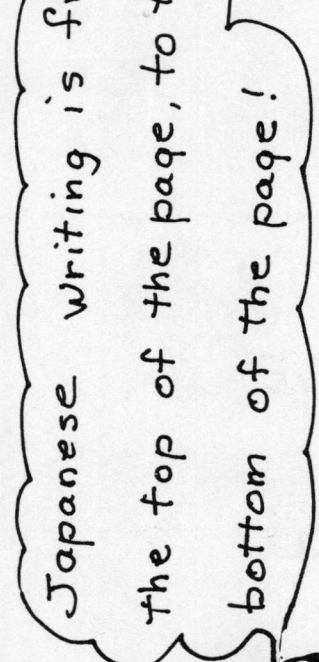

KANJI Characters

Number	Romaji	Kanji
1	ichi	一
2	ni	二
3	san	三
4	shi	四
5	go	五
6	roku	六
7	shichi	七
8	hachi	八
9	kyū	九
10	jū	十
11	jū ichi	十一
15	jū go	十五
26	ni jū roku	二十六
100	hyaku	百
2000	nisen	二千

You have learned how to say these numbers. Now — can you write them?

Japanese writing is from the top of the page, to the bottom of the page!

How old are you?

PRACTICE PAGE

Practice writing the numbers.
Follow the arrows with your finger.
Make the numbers in the air, then write them on paper.

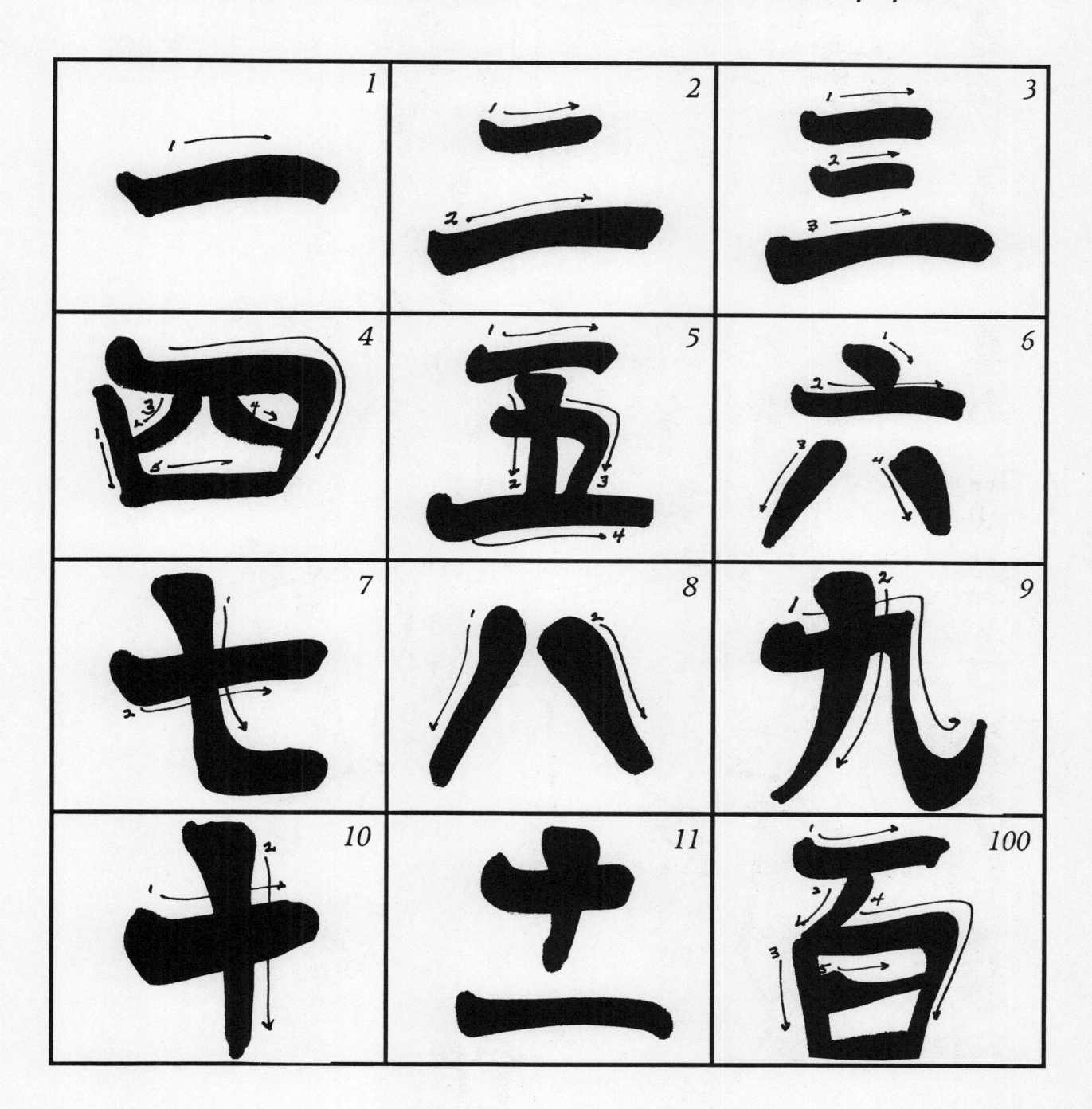

1	2	3
一	二	三
4	**5**	**6**
四	五	六
7	**8**	**9**
七	八	九
10	**11**	**100**
十	十一	百

FOLLOW-THE-DOTS

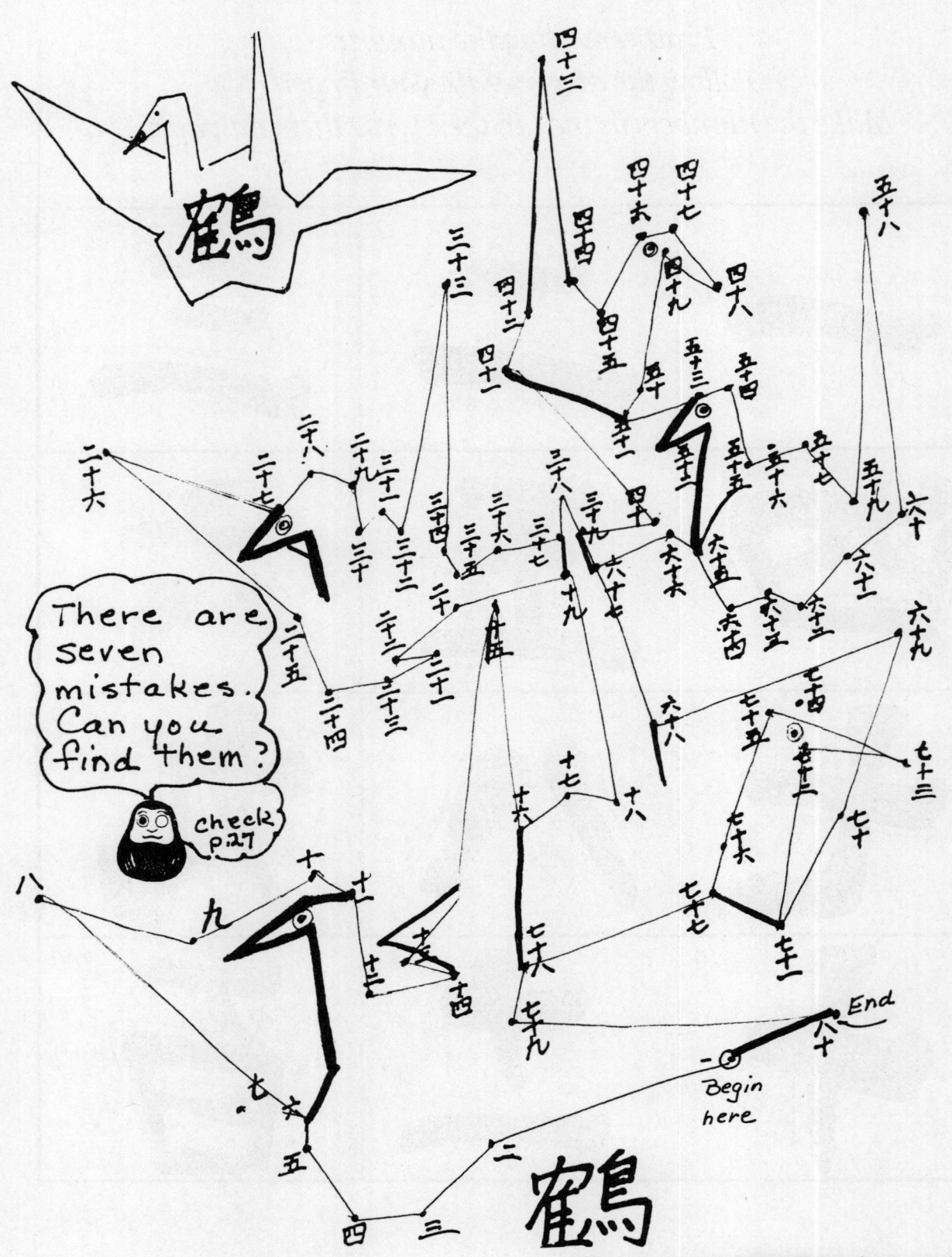

There are seven mistakes. Can you find them?

check p.27

How many TSURU (cranes) are there in this picture?

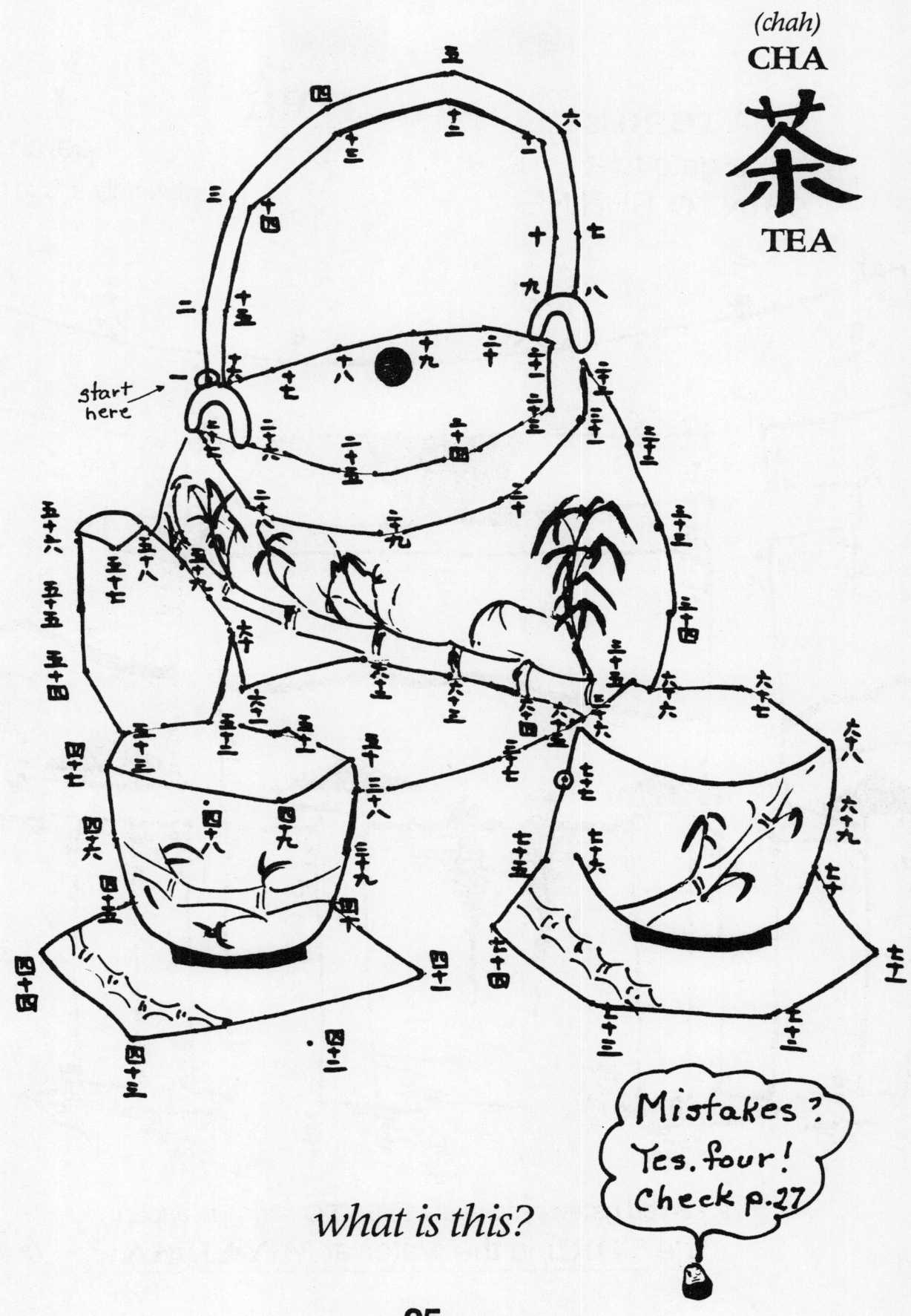

FOLLOW-THE-DOTS

(chah)
CHA
茶
TEA

what is this?

Mistakes? Yes, four! Check p. 27

FOLLOW-THE-DOTS

A **TORII** is
a gate to a
SHINTŌ SHRINE

(toh–ree)
TORI
bird

(ee)
I
perch
(Literally a 'bird's' perch)

A sacred gateway to every **SHINTŌ** shrine in Japan.
The **TORII** in the water at **MIYAJIMA**

see (p. 129)

FOLLOW-THE-DOTS

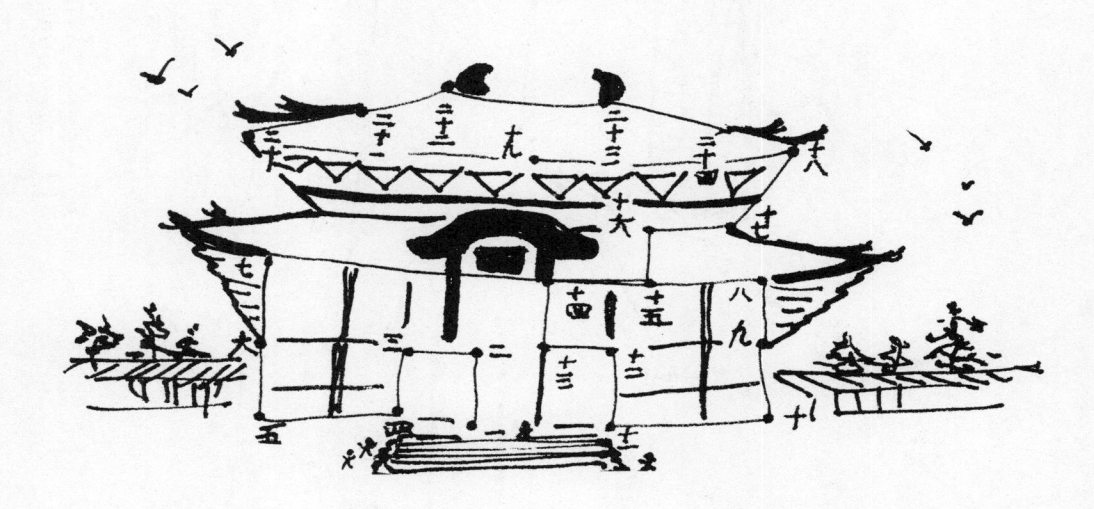

This is the oldest wooden building in the world! It is the **TODAIJI TEMPLE** in **NARA**, Japan's capital from 710 AD to 784 AD. There is a huge **BUDDHA** inside the temple! *page 129*

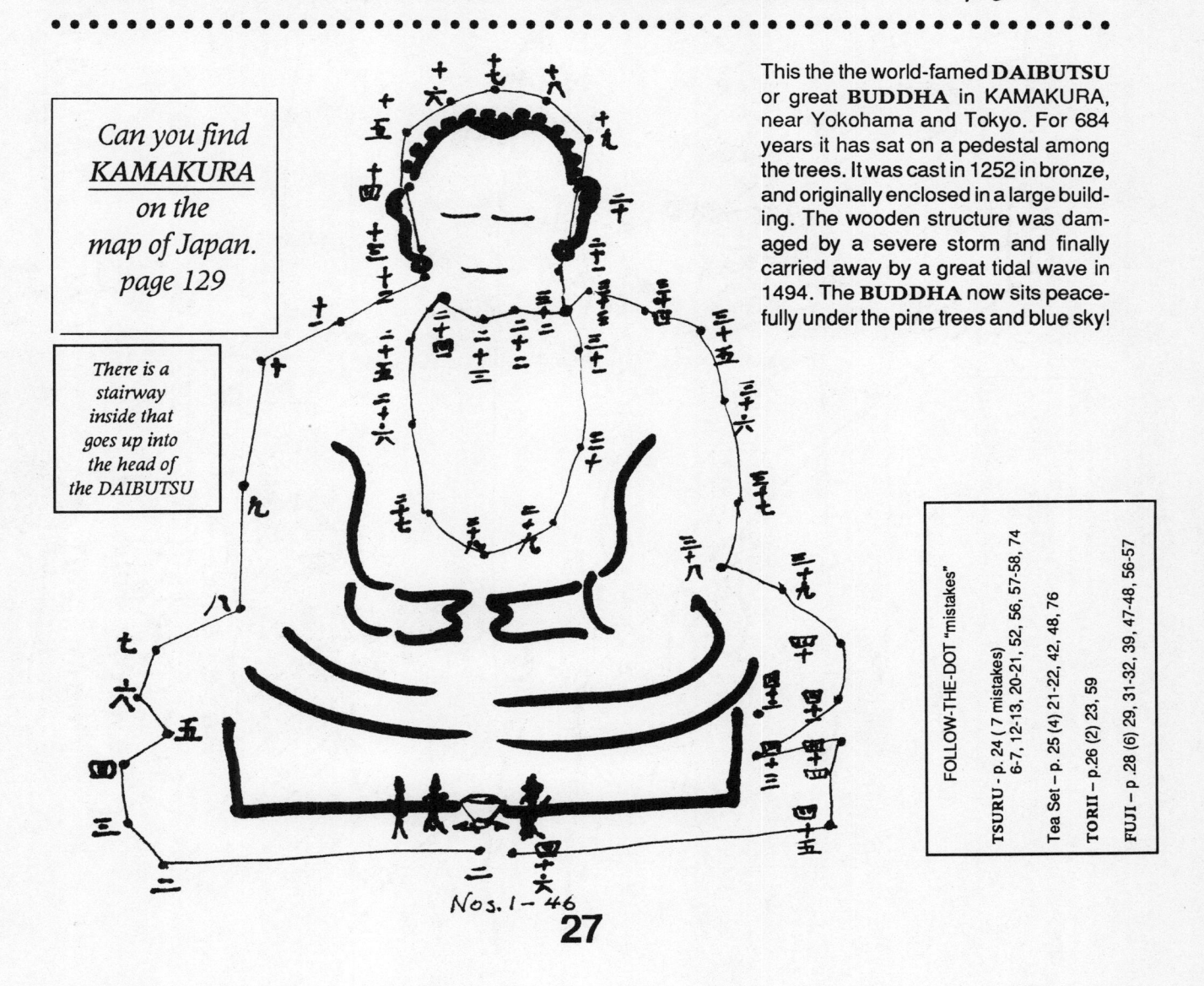

• •

Can you find <u>KAMAKURA</u> on the map of Japan. page 129

There is a stairway inside that goes up into the head of the DAIBUTSU

This the the world-famed **DAIBUTSU** or great **BUDDHA** in **KAMAKURA**, near Yokohama and Tokyo. For 684 years it has sat on a pedestal among the trees. It was cast in 1252 in bronze, and originally enclosed in a large building. The wooden structure was damaged by a severe storm and finally carried away by a great tidal wave in 1494. The **BUDDHA** now sits peacefully under the pine trees and blue sky!

FOLLOW-THE-DOT "mistakes"

TSURU - p. 24 (7 mistakes) 6-7, 12-13, 20-21, 52, 56, 57-58, 74

Tea Set - p. 25 (4) 21-22, 42, 48, 76

TORII - p.26 (2) 23, 59

FUJI - p .28 (6) 29, 31-32, 39, 47-48, 56-57

Nos. 1 – 46

27

FOLLOW-THE-DOTS

FUJIYAMA — Mt. FUJI — FUJI SAN

Check page 129

There are five 'goofs'! Can you find them?

Chapter 4

How KANJI developed.

More KANJI.

Easy KANJI to learn . . .

and more KANJI!

KANJI game.

MONTHS in Japanese.

DAYS of the week in Japanese.

- KANJI for FISH.
- KANJI for HORSE.
- KANJI for BIRD.
- KANJI for CROW.

"You-read" KANJI story.

(kahn–jee noh)
KANJI NO

(deh–kee–kah–tah)
DEKIKATA

漢字のできかた 日本

KAN JI NO DE KI KA TA

KANJI HOW THEY DEVELOPED

How KANJI developed

KANJI were originally *Chinese characters* – but several Asian countries use them also – including Japan.

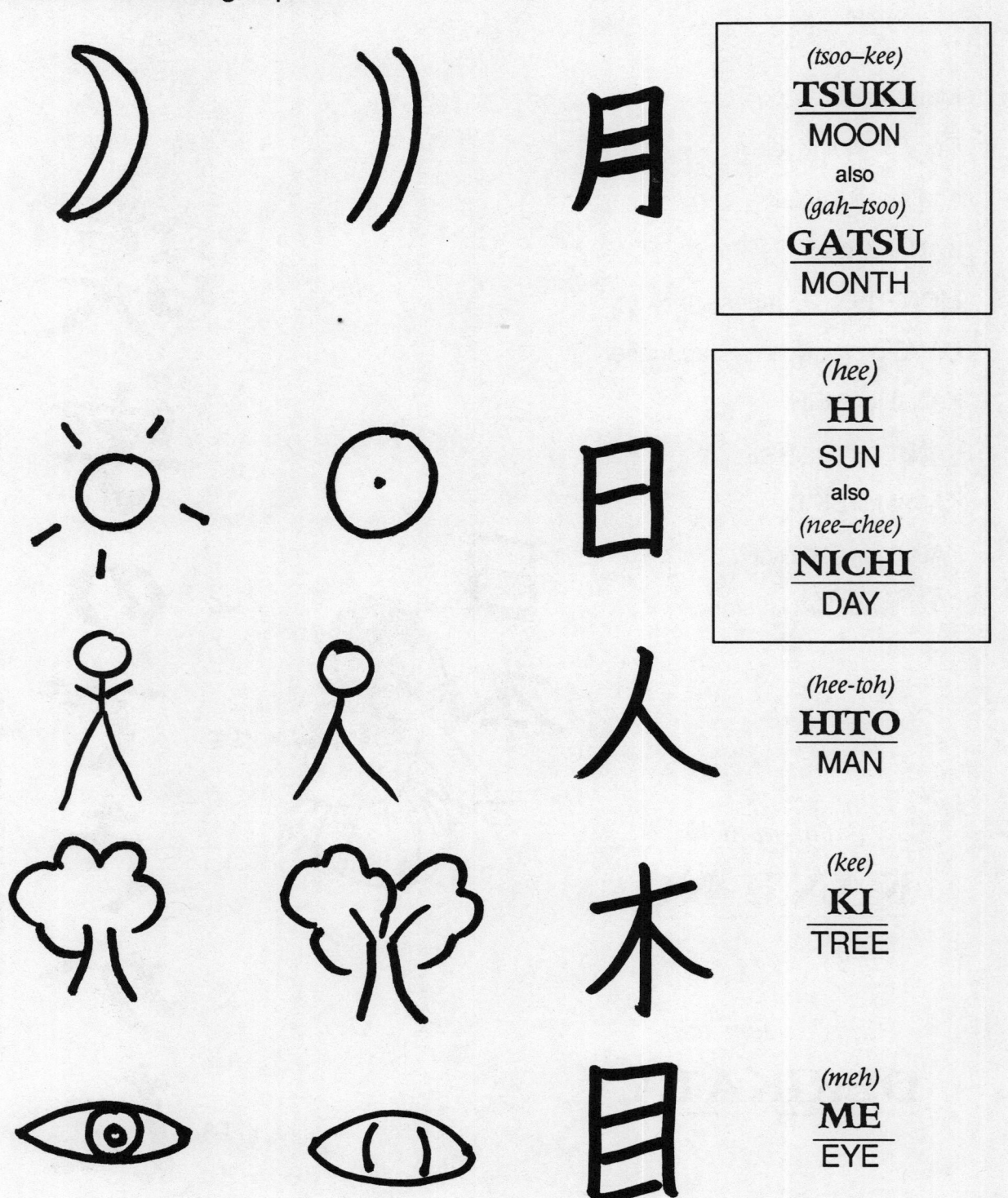

月
| *(tsoo–kee)* |
| **TSUKI** |
| MOON |
| also |
| *(gah–tsoo)* |
| **GATSU** |
| MONTH |

日
| *(hee)* |
| **HI** |
| SUN |
| also |
| *(nee–chee)* |
| **NICHI** |
| DAY |

人
(hee-toh)
HITO
MAN

木
(kee)
KI
TREE

目
(meh)
ME
EYE

MORE KANJI

(More Chinese Characters)

This is a TREE

This is a FOREST

Do many trees make a big forest?

This is the way you write "tree" in Japanese.

You must follow numbers

(one 'tree' is just a 'tree')

(kee)
KI

a tree

木

('3 trees' make a 'forest')

(moh–ree)
MORI

big forest

森

('2 trees' make a 'small woods')

(hah–yah–shee)
HAYASHI

small woods

林

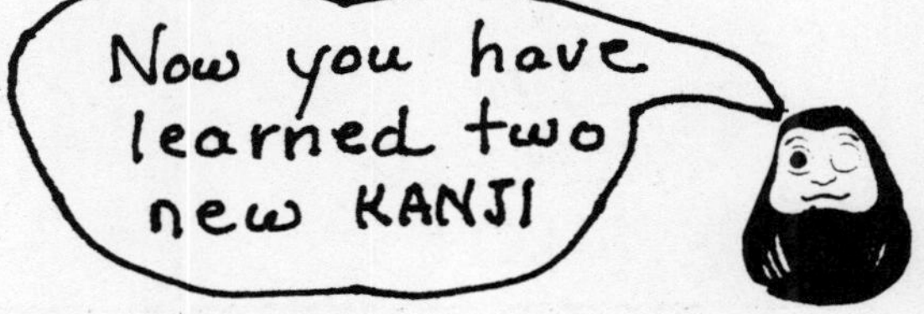

Now you have learned two new KANJI

31

Can you write these easy
KANJI

Do the KANJI look like the pictures?
You must follow the numbers.

(hee–toh) **HITO** / PERSON	stick figure	人
(kah-wah) **KAWA** / RIVER	wavy lines	川
(hee) **HI** / FIRE	fire	火
(mee–zoo) **MIZU** / WATER	dripping water	水
(koo–chee) **KUCHI** / MOUTH	mouth	口
(tah) **TA** / RICE FIELD PADDY	rice paddy	田

32

MORE KANJI

(koo–roo–mah) **KURUMA** CAR		車
(hee) **HI** – SUN and **NICHI** – Day		日
(yah–mah) **YAMA** MOUNTAIN		山
(meh) **ME** EYE		目
(tsoo–kee) **TSUKI** – MOON AND **GATSU** – MONTH		月
(hohn) **HON** BOOK		本

MORE KANJI
(You must follow numbers)

(ah–shee) **ASHI** FOOT		足
(mee–mee) **MIMI** EAR		耳
(teh) **TE** HAND		手
(ōh–kee) **ŌKI** BIG		大
(oht–toh) **OTTO** HUSBAND		夫
(ohn–nah) **ONNA** WOMAN		女
(koh–meh) **KOME** RICE (Not cooked)		米

Here's a little game for you.

Match the KANJI to the picture

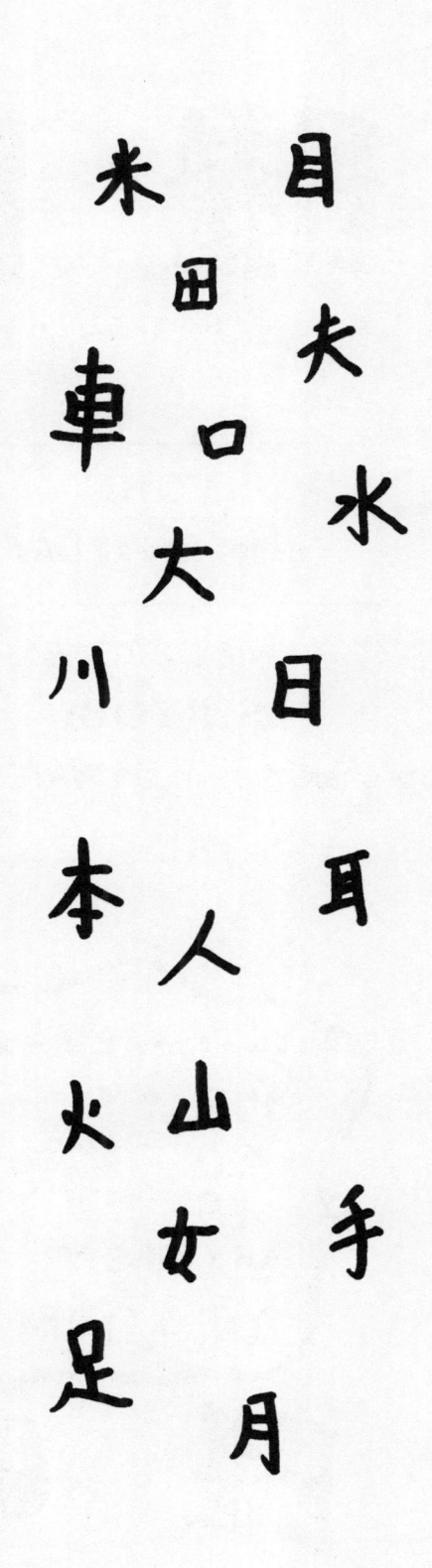

目 夫 水 耳 手
田 口 日
車 口 大
川 本 人 山 女 月
火
足
米

35

DAYS OF THE WEEK

You have learned all these KANJI . . . EXCEPT for three.
Can you find the three new ones?

MONDAY . . . moon day . . . *(geh-tsoo-yoh-bee)* **GETSUYŌBI**

TUESDAY . . . fire day . . . *(kah-yoh-bee)* **KAYŌBI**

WEDNESDAY . . . water day . . . *(soo-ee-yoh-bee)* **SUIYŌBI**

THURSDAY . . . wood day . . . *(moh-koh-yoh-bee)* **MOKUYŌBI**

FRIDAY . . . gold day . . . *(keen-yoh-bee)* **KINYŌBI**

SATURDAY . . . earth day . . . *(doh-yoh-bee)* **DOYŌBI**

SUNDAY . . . day day . . . *(nee-chee-yoh-bee)* **NICHIYOBI**

月 火 水 木 金 土 日

曜 日
YŌ BI

YŌBI
is the word for DAY

WEDNESDAY is
SUIYŌBI
the characters mean WATER DAY!

The three new KANJI are —
KIN — gold
DO — earth
and the difficult
YŌ in YŌBI

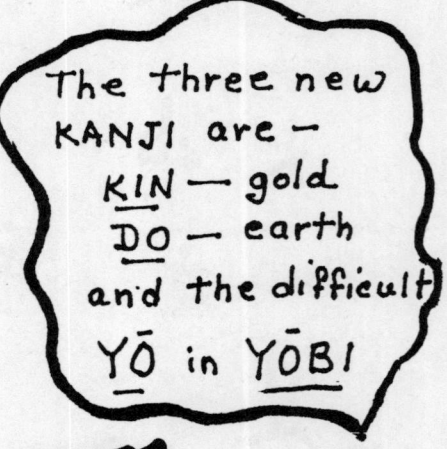

曜

36

MONTHS IN JAPANESE

Can you write the months in Japanese?
Just add the **KANJI** 月 for month to a number 1 – 12! It's easy!

January ICHI GATSU 一月	February NI GATSU 二月	March SAN GATSU 三月
April SHI GATSU 四月	May GO GATSU 五月	June ROKU GATSU 六月
July SHICHI GATSU 七月	August HACHI GATSU 八月	September KŪ GATSU 九月
October JŪ GATSU 十月	November JŪ ICHI GATSU 十一月	December JŪ NI GATSU 十二月

(kahn–jee)
KANJI
Chinese Characters

FISH is <u>SAKANA</u>

Japanese and Chinese cannot understand one another . . . when they talk . . . but they can understand the same **KANJI** characters. They mean the same . . . but are pronounced differently in each county.

Next time you go to a Chinese restaurant, write this **KANJI** for *FISH* on the paper napkin! Look at the waiter's face! What a surprise! What will he say? How do the Chinese say fish? The Japanese say **SAKANA** (*sah–kah–nah*). Follow the numbers.

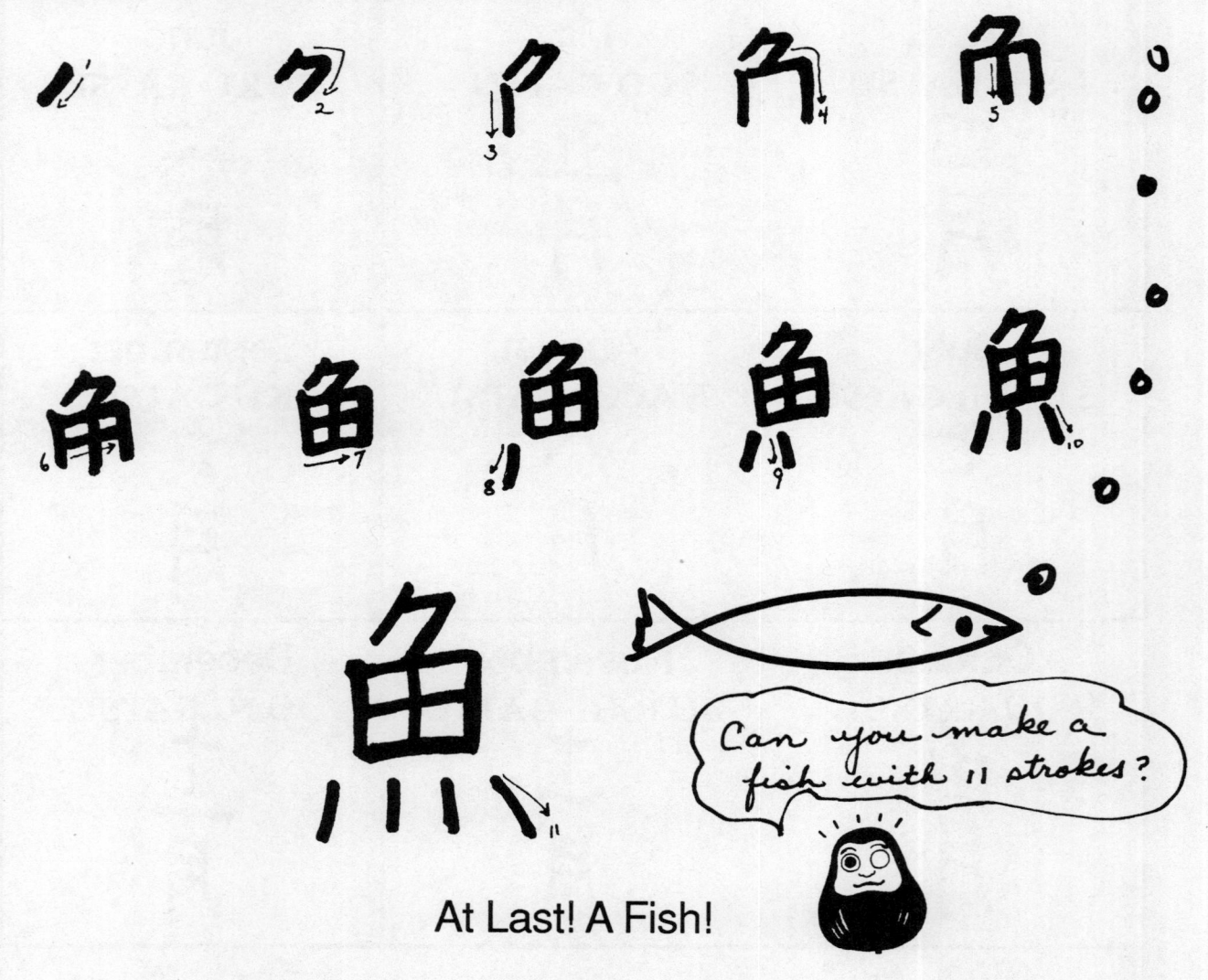

Can you make a fish with 11 strokes?

At Last! A Fish!

38

Now try to write the KANJI for HORSE

(oo–mah)
UMA

丨 厂 冂

开 严 馬

馬 馬 馬 馬

uma desu

hana desu

Does it look like a running horse?

馬

At last – A horse
UMA

(toh–ree)
TORI
is a BIRD

TORI DESU

At last – A bird!

It takes 11 strokes to make a bird!

This looks like a bird, doesn't it?

40

Is a CROW a BIRD?

(kah–rah–soo)
KARASU

(toh–ree)
TORI

In Japan, as in other parts of the world, crows eat the farmer's seeds, and the farmers don't like them!

So... let's pull a feather out of the **KANJI** for **TORI** (bird)... or remove a stroke! Now you have the **KANJI** for **KARASU** (crow)! Is a crow a bird? See if you can write the **KANJI**...

BIRD 鳥   **CROW** 烏

ouch!

On page 24 see if you can find the **KANJI** for BIRD?

KANJI STORY

This is a story about 魚, a 夫 and his wife. Next to their house was a 田. One day the 夫 said, "I am going to the 山 to cut some 木. I promise I will catch some 魚. It is 六月, and I think it will be a nice 日." He hitched his 馬 to the 車 and started out for the 川 near the 山. The 日 was shining. He saw a 木 by the 川. He decided to let his 馬 drink some of the 水 while he rested under the 木. "Oh! It's so hot. My 口 feels like 火, and my 目 are so dry. The 鳥 are singing in the 木, and the 魚 are jumping in the 川! But, my 足 are so tired. I think I will rest under the 木 and read my 本 for just 十 minutes. 六月 is always so wonderful." His 目 were heavy. Soon he fell asleep. When he awoke the 月 was coming up over the 山 top, and the 鳥 were gone. Even the 魚 seemed to have left the 川. I must hurry back to my 女 and 田. "Oh, dear! No 魚! My wife won't believe her 耳! I promised I would catch some 魚." He took a shortcut through the 森 and over the 川. He saw 三女 and 一男 cleaning 魚. "Is there a tea shop here? My 足 are sore and my 口 is dry!" "No", they replied, "but there is a wonderful 魚 store nearby. It has fresh 魚 every 日 from the 川 that runs near the 林. Maybe the store will have some 魚." Fresh 魚! Fresh 魚! The 夫 was excited. He clapped his 手. **"Now I won't have to break a promise!"**

What do you think the man told his wife about his 'fresh fish'? 男
This is a new KANJI for MAN.

42

Chapter 5
SIMPLE PHRASES

It is. Is it?

Who, What, Where, When, Why

My face.

Weather.

Yesterday, tomorrow, today.

Seasons.

Like, dislike, very much.

Colors.

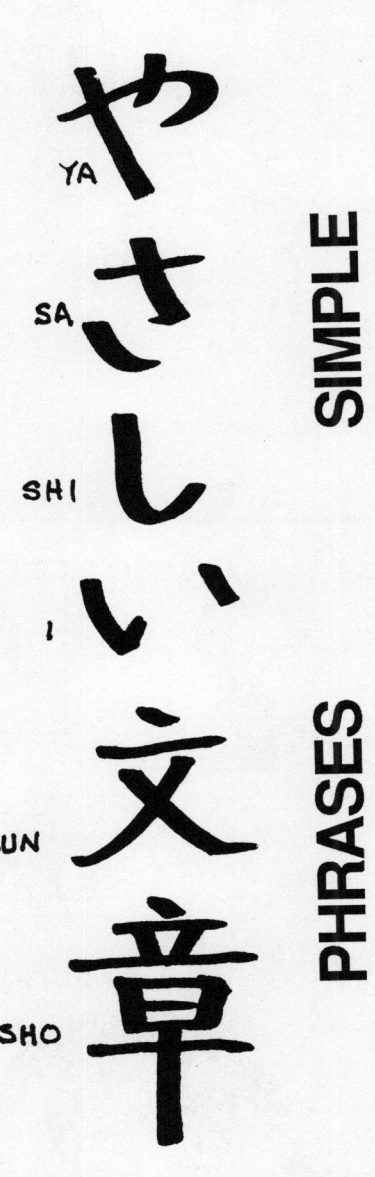

(yah–sah–shee–ee)
YASASHII
SIMPLE

(boon–shōh)
BUNSHŌ
PHRASES

やさしい文章

YA SA SHI I BUN SHO

SIMPLE PHRASES

DESU – IT IS
(dehss)

DESU KA – IS IT?
(dehss–kah)

?

ORENJI DESU KA?
(oh–rehn–jee   dehss   kah)

Is it an orange, or are they oranges?

IIE, RINGO DESU
(ee–eh   reen–goh   dehss)

No, it's an apple.
or
No, they are apples.

?

DARE – WHO
(dah reh)

DARE DESU KA?
(dah reh   dehss   kah?)

Who is it?   It's **HARUKO**.
Who are you?

HARUKO — HAI, HARU DESU

TAKU — DARE DESU KA? HARUKO DESU KA?

44

? NAN ? NANI?
(nahn) *(nahn–nee)*
WHAT

NAN DESU KA?
What is it?

(bah–nah–nah)
BANANA DESU
It's a banana or they are bananas.
(There is no difference between singular and plural!)

BANANA DESU

(doh koh)
DOKO – WHERE

DOKO DESU KA?
Where are you?
or
Where is it?

KOKO – HERE

KOKO DESU
Here I am.

? *(ee–tsoo)* ITSU – WHEN

(ee–tsoo kee–mahss kah)
ITSU KIMASU KA?
When are you coming?

IMA = now

(ee–mah)
IMA KIMASU
I'm coming now.

? *(dōh–sh–teh)* DŌSHITE – WHY

(doh–shteh kee–mahss kah?)
DŌSHITE KIMASU KA?
Why are you coming?

WATASHI NO TANJŌBI DESU!
It's my birthday!

46

(kah–oh)
KAO – Face

(wah–tah–shee noh kah–oh)

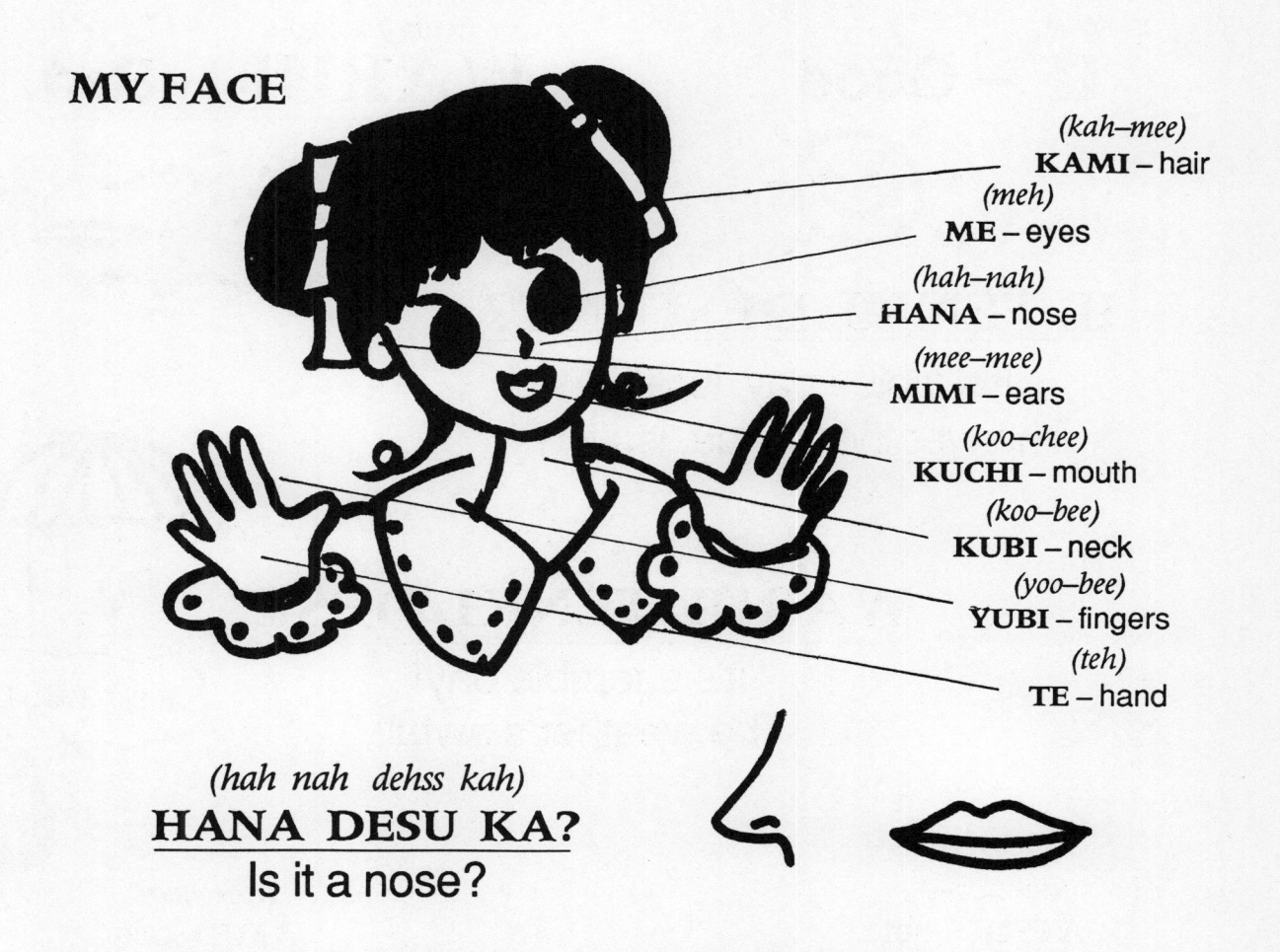

MY FACE

(kah–mee)
KAMI – hair

(meh)
ME – eyes

(hah–nah)
HANA – nose

(mee–mee)
MIMI – ears

(koo–chee)
KUCHI – mouth

(koo–bee)
KUBI – neck

(yoo–bee)
YUBI – fingers

(teh)
TE – hand

(hah nah dehss kah)
HANA DESU KA?
Is it a nose?

IIE, ME DESU.
No, its an eye.

KUCHI DESU KA?
Is this a mouth?

HAI, KUCHI DESU.
Yes, it is a mouth

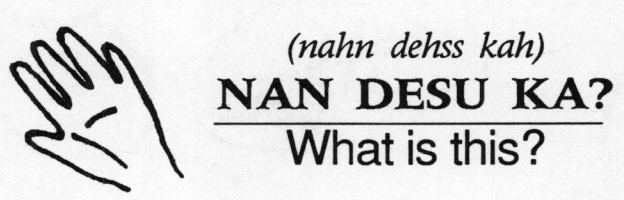

(nahn dehss kah)
NAN DESU KA?
What is this?

(tehn kee)
TENKI Weather
or OTENKI

(ee)
II – Good

(wah–roo–ee)
WARUI – Bad

II TENKI DESU NE?

It's a nice day, isn't it?
The weather's nice, isn't it?

WARUI TENKI DESU

It's a terrible day!
The weather's awful!

AME DESU

(ah–tsoo–ee)
ATSUI = hot
(sah–moo–ee)
SAMUI = cold

(ah–meh)
AME = rain
(yoo–kee)
YUKI = snow

SAMUI DESU

OH! IT'S COLD

A snowman in U.S.A.

A Japanese snowman has only two big snow balls!

YESTERDAY TODAY TOMORROW
This is how the tulips look

(kee–nōh) **KINŌ** YESTERDAY

(kee–yōh) **KYŌ** TODAY

(ah–sh(ee)tah) **ASHITA** TOMORROW

KYŌ *wah nahn yōh–bee dehss kah?*
WA NAN YOBI DESU KA?
What day is today?

ASHITA WA GETSUYŌBI DESU.
Tomorrow will be Monday.

KINŌ WA DOYŌBI DESHITA
Yesterday was Saturday.

On which day is Thanksgiving?

On which day is Easter?

On which day is Labor Day?

SEASONS

(hah-roo)
HARU
Spring

(nah-tsoo)
NATSU
Summer

(ah-kee)
AKI
Autumn

(foo-yoo)
FUYU
Winter

50

(ss–kee)
or
(soo–kee)
SUKI
LIKE

(dah–ee)
DAI
VERY

(kee–rah–ee)
KIRAI
DISLIKE

(ah–ee–soo–koo–rēē–moo)
AISUKURĪMU
ice cream

AISUKURĪMU GA SUKI DESU KA?
Do you like ice cream?

hah–ee dah–ee soo–kee deh–ss
HAI, DAI SUKI DESU
Yes, I love it very much.

(hahm–bāh–gāh)
HAMBĀGĀ

HAMBĀGĀ GA KIRAI DESU KA?
Do you dislike hamburgers?

(ee–roh)
IRO
COLOR

(ah–kah)
AKA
RED

(mee–doh–ree)
MIDORI
GREEN

(shee–roh)
SHIRO
WHITE

(kee–ee–roh)
KIIRO
YELLOW

(koo–roh)
KURO
BLACK

(ah–oh)
AO
BLUE

Add "i" to make an adjective.

AKAI RINGO
a red apple

KIIROI
a yellow flower

KUROI HON
a black book

Can you write these colors?
A white snowman — A blue sky

Chapter 6

Writing in Japanese four ways!

#1 **ROMAJI**

#2 **HIRAGANA** Chart
   Learn to write in **HIRAGANA**.

#3 **KATAKANA** Chart
   For foreign words and names.

#4 **KANJI** (Chinese Characters)
   Check Chapter 4 for simple **KANJI**.

   MOMOTARŌ (Little Peach Boy) in English
   (the way the Japanese read).

   MOMOTARŌ in Japanese **HIRAGANA**
   (the way the Japanese would read).

   PHOTOS – Pretty Kimonos and the Fan Dance.

四つの日本語の書き方

YO — FOUR
TSU
NO
NI — JAPANESE
HON
GO
NO
KA — WAYS OF WRITING
KI
KATA

FOUR WAYS TO WRITE

Learning to write in the Japanese language is a little more difficult than learning to write in English. There are four – **yes, four** – different types of writing! We will use the word **YAMA** – mountain as an example.

A ⛰ is a "yama".

(p. 55-56)
1. ROMAJI ... *(roh–mah–jee)*: Our alphabet: A – B – C . . . Z, is often used to write the Japanese phonetic sounds. For example, a cup is a **koppu**, a taxi is a **takushi**, slippers are **surippa**! (Always break down Japanese words into syllables. **TAKUSHI** would be **ta – ku – shi**), KIMBERLY would be **Ki – mu – ba –ri**! JUSTIN would be **Ja – su – ti – n**!

[YA/MA]

(p. 57-60)
2. HIRAGANA ... *(hee–rah–gah–nah)*: 51 simple one, two or three stroke characters, used just for phonetic sounds. These are often used in combination with each other to make additional sounds! **HIRAGANA** can be used for writing anything, or it may be used in combination with **KATAKANA** and **KANJI**. Children start learning **HIRAGANA** in first grade.

[や/ま YA/MA]

(p. 61-62)
3. KATAKANA ... *(kah–tah–kah–nah)*: 51 characters, usually just one or two strokes. These are used only for foreign words and names. Children also learn these characters in first grade.

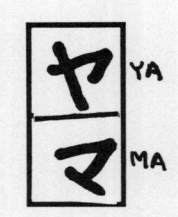

[ヤ/マ YA/MA]

(p. 63)
4. KANJI ... *(kahn–jee)*: These are Chinese characters. There are thousands of **KANJI**! Some have one or two strokes, and some have as many as twenty . . . or more! (How many strokes are there in the **KANJI** for **TSURU** on p 24? I can count 21!) By high school Japanese children have learned over 600 **KANJI**, as well as the **HIRAGANA** and **KATAKANA**. Children start to learn simple **KANJI** in first grade. There are 1,850 **KANJI** in common everyday use in Japan, and many thousand more that are less common.

[山 YAMA]

And you think ENGLISH is difficult?

1 ROMAJI

In Japan these are the words you would use.
Can you recognize them?

(U is pronounced like oo in zoo)
Remember to break the words into syllables for easy pronunciation Example: E – PU – RO – N

TEREBI
(teh reh bee)

NEKUTAI
(neh koo tah ee)

MIRUKU
(mee roo koo)

EPURON
(eh poo rohn)

BATTO ... BŌRU
(bah toh ... bōh roo)

SURIPPA
(soo rēe pah)

FURAIPAN
(foo rah ee pahn)

KOPPU
(kōh poo)

TAKUSHĪ
(tah koo shēe)

TAORU
(tah oh roo)

HANBĀGĀ
(hanh bāh gāh)

HOTTO DŌGGU
(hoh toh dōh goo)

55

1 – ROMAJI

Can you pronounce these words?
(*U* is pronounced like *oo* in *zoo*)

In Japan this is how you would pronounce these words

PEN
(peh n)

TORAKKU
(toh rāh koo)

BEDDO
(behd doh)

SĒTĀ
(seh tāh)

BASU
(bah soo)

CHURIPPU
choo–ree–poo

TOIRE
(toy deh)

TEBURU
(teh boo roo)

NAIFU
(nah ee foo)

SUPŪN
(soo poo n)

FŌKU
(hoh koo)

PAJAMA
(pah jah mah)

HOTTOKĒKI
(hoh toh kēh kee)

2 – HIRAGANA CHART

Children learn these **HIRAGANA** symbols first.

These are used only for Japanese words; not foreign words or foreign names.

A fun way to learn these sounds is to say them in order. From top left to right (first five sounds) then the second line – left to right
A – I – U – E – O – ka – ki – ku – ke – ko – sa – shi – su – se – so – etc.
(AH – EE – OO – EH – OH, KAH – KEE – KOO – KEH – KOH, SAH – SHEE – SOO – SEH – SOH)

	a	ee	oo	eh	oh			a	ee	oo	eh	oh
	A	I	U	E	O			A	I	U	E	O
A	あ (A)	い (I)	う (U)	え (E)	お (O)							
K	か (KA)	き (KI)	く (KU)	け (KE)	こ (KO)		G	が (GA)	ぎ (GI)	ぐ (GU)	げ (GE)	ご (GO)
S	さ (SA)	し (SHI)	す (SU)	せ (SE)	そ (SO)		Z	ざ (ZA)	じ (ZI)	ず (ZU)	ぜ (ZE)	ぞ (ZO)
T	た (TA)	ち (CHI)	つ (TSU)	て (TE)	と (TO)		D	だ (DA)	ぢ (JI)	づ (ZU)	で (DE)	ど (DO)
N	な (NA)	に (NI)	ぬ (NU)	ね (NE)	の (NO)							
H	は (HA)	ひ (HI)	ふ (HU)	へ (HE)	ほ (HO)		B	ば (BA)	び (BI)	ぶ (BU)	べ (BE)	ぼ (BO)
M	ま (MA)	み (MI)	む (MU)	め (ME)	も (MO)		P	ぱ (PA)	ぴ (PI)	ぷ (PU)	ぺ (PE)	ぽ (PO)
Y	や (YA)		ゆ (YU)		よ (YO)							
R	ら (RA)	り (RI)	る (RU)	れ (RE)	ろ (RO)							
W	わ (WA)		を (O)		ん (N)							

Children learn these HIRAGANA symbols in first grade.

2 HIRAGANA (cont')

You learned these words in **KANJI** – (on page 38, 39, 40)
now write them in **HIRAGANA**.
(follow the stroke arrows)

SAKANA
FISH

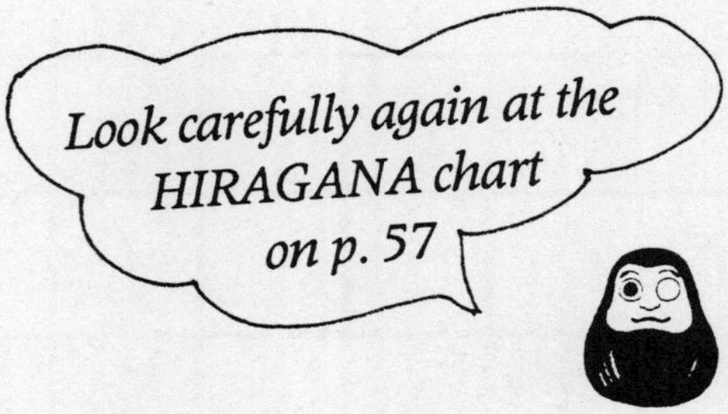

SA　さ
KA　か
NA　な

Look carefully again at the HIRAGANA chart on p. 57

TORI
BIRD

*Little children learn to write **HIRAGANA** first – and gradually learn **KANJI**.*

TO　と
RI　り

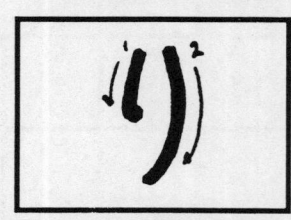

UMA
HORSE

NOW YOU TRY TO WRITE THESE WORDS

U　う
MA　ま

58

2 HIRAGANA

Here are some words you will find in this book – written in **HIRAGANA.** *(Read from left to right).*

Crane	**TSURU**
Sparrow	**SUZUME**
Eggs	**TAMAGO**
Rice (raw)	**KOME**
Rice (cooked)	**GOHAN**
Cherry blossom	**SAKURA**
Sky	**SORA**
Pigeon	**HATO**
Tortoise	**KAME**
Flower	**HANA**
Nose	**HANA**
Paper fold	**ORIGAMI**
Kimono	**KIMONO**
Song	**UTA**
Peach	**MOMO**

HE – NO – HE – NO – MO – HE – JI   FACE!

Japanese children like to make this funny face out of **HIRAGANA** characters.

pronounce it this way

(heh–noh–heh–noh–moh–heh–jee)

It is a HE–NO–HE–NO–MO–HE–JI face.

へ = HE   の = NO   も = MO   じ = JI

*Can you find these sounds on the **HIRAGANA** chart?*

SHI し becomes JI じ when you add two small strokes ˝

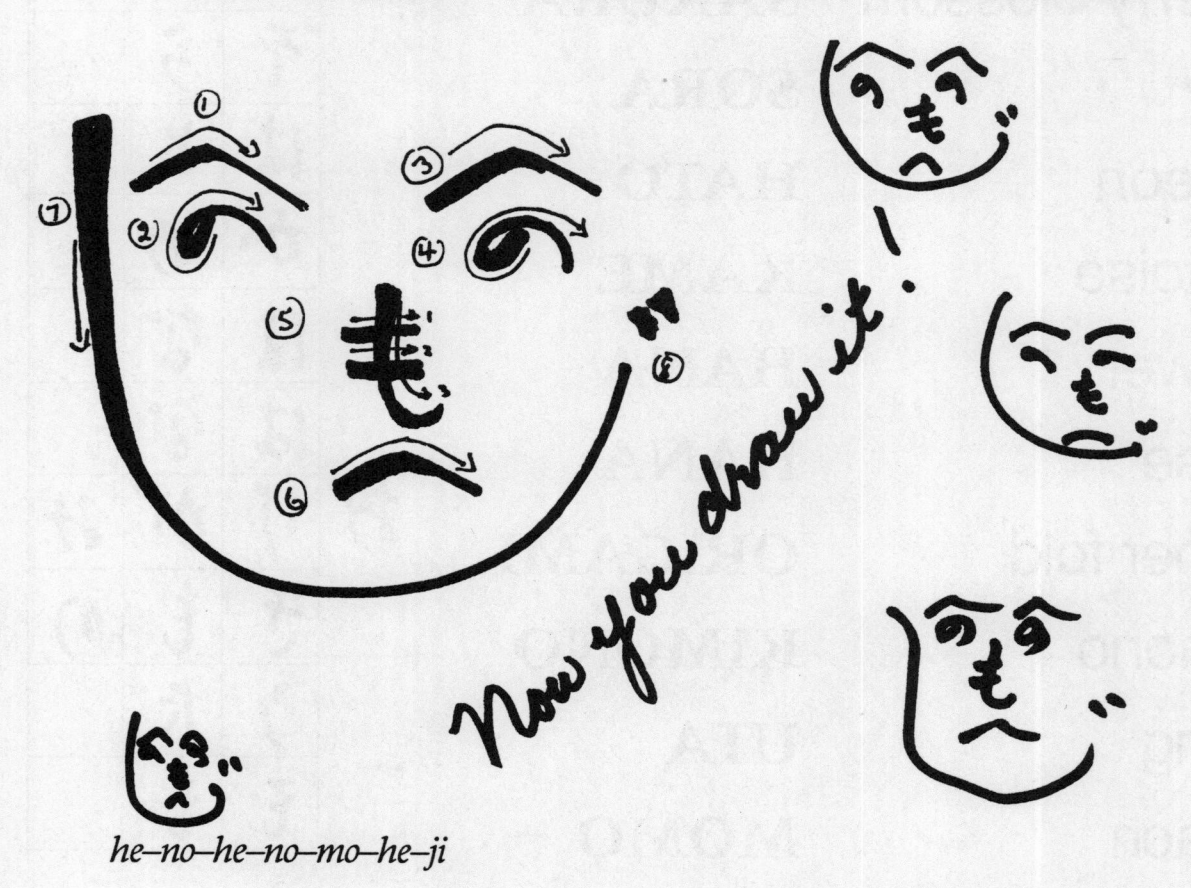

Now you draw it!

he-no-he-no-mo-he-ji

3 KATAKANA CHART

You must use **KATAKANA** for foreign names and words.

pronounce this way:

	a	ee	oo	eh	oh			a	ee	oo	eh	oh
	A	**I**	**U**	**E**	**O**			**A**	**I**	**U**	**E**	**O**
A	ア (A)	イ (I)	ウ (U)	エ (E)	オ (O)							
K	カ (KA)	キ (KI)	ク (KU)	ケ (KE)	コ (KO)		**G**	が (GA)	ギ (GI)	グ (GU)	ゲ (GE)	ゴ (GO)
S	サ (SA)	シ (SHI)	ス (SU)	セ (SE)	ソ (SO)		**Z**	ザ (ZA)	ジ (ZI)	ズ (ZU)	ゼ (ZE)	ゾ (ZO)
T	タ (TA)	チ (CHI)	ツ (TSU)	テ (TE)	ト (TO)		**D**	ダ (DA)	ヂ (JI)	ヅ (ZU)	デ (DE)	ド (DO)
N	ナ (NA)	ニ (NI)	ヌ (NU)	ネ (NE)	ノ (NO)							
H	ハ (HA)	ヒ (HI)	フ (HU)	ヘ (HE)	ホ (HO)		**B**	バ (BA)	ビ (BI)	ブ (BU)	ベ (BE)	ボ (BO)
M	マ (MA)	ミ (MI)	ム (MU)	メ (ME)	モ (MO)		**P**	パ (PA)	ピ (PI)	プ (PU)	ペ (PE)	ポ (PO)
Y	ヤ (YA)		ユ (YU)		ヨ (YO)							
R	ラ (RA)	リ (RI)	ル (RU)	レ (RE)	ロ (RO)							
W	ワ (WA)	**O** ヲ (O)		**N** ン (N)								

Andrea would become A–N–DO–RE–A.

Smith becomes SU–MI–SU.

アンドレア
スミス

> Divide your name into syllables – and find the matching **KATAKANA** characters from the chart above.

61

3 – KATAKANA

Foreign words and names

Read from top to bottom.

America — ア(A) メ(ME) リ(RI) カ(KA)

Television — テ(TE) レ(RE) ビ(BI)

Seattle — シ ア ト ル

Slipper — ス(SU) リ(RI) ッ(I) パ(PA)

Thomas — ト(TO) マ(MA) ス(SU)

Alice — ア(A) リ(RI) ス(SU)

Taxi — タ(TA) ク(KU) シ(SHI) ー

Milk — ミ(MI) ル(RU) ク(KU)

Pajama — パ(PA) ジャ(JA) マ(MA)

Spoon — ス(SU) プ(PU) ー ン(N)

Towel — タ(TA) オ ル(RU)

Apron — エ(E) プ(PU) ロ(RO) ン(N)

Jeff — ジェ フ

62

4 – KANJI

This is the fourth way to write in Japanese. Can you remember these KANJI?

Mouth	口	Foot	足
Bird	鳥	Book	本
River	川	Tree	木
Mountain	山	Eye	目
Forest	森	Horse	馬
Moon	月	Water	水
Person	人	Fire	火

If you have forgotten your KANJI – check Chapter 4

STORY OF MOMOTARŌ

In English and HIRAGANA

"Little Peach Boy"

ももたろう
MO MO TA RO O

*Read from the top to the bottom, and from right to left.
Does that seem peculiar to you?*

The complete story is on page 98

Once upon a time long ago an old man and an old woman lived in a quiet mountain village. One day the old man went to the mountain to gather wood and the old woman went to wash her clothes. While she was scrubbing her clothes, she saw a big peach come floating down the river.

Do your eyes hurt? This is how the Japanese read.

Turn to the next page and see how the story looks in Japanese.

64

MOMOTARŌ IN HIRAGANA

"The Little Peach Boy"

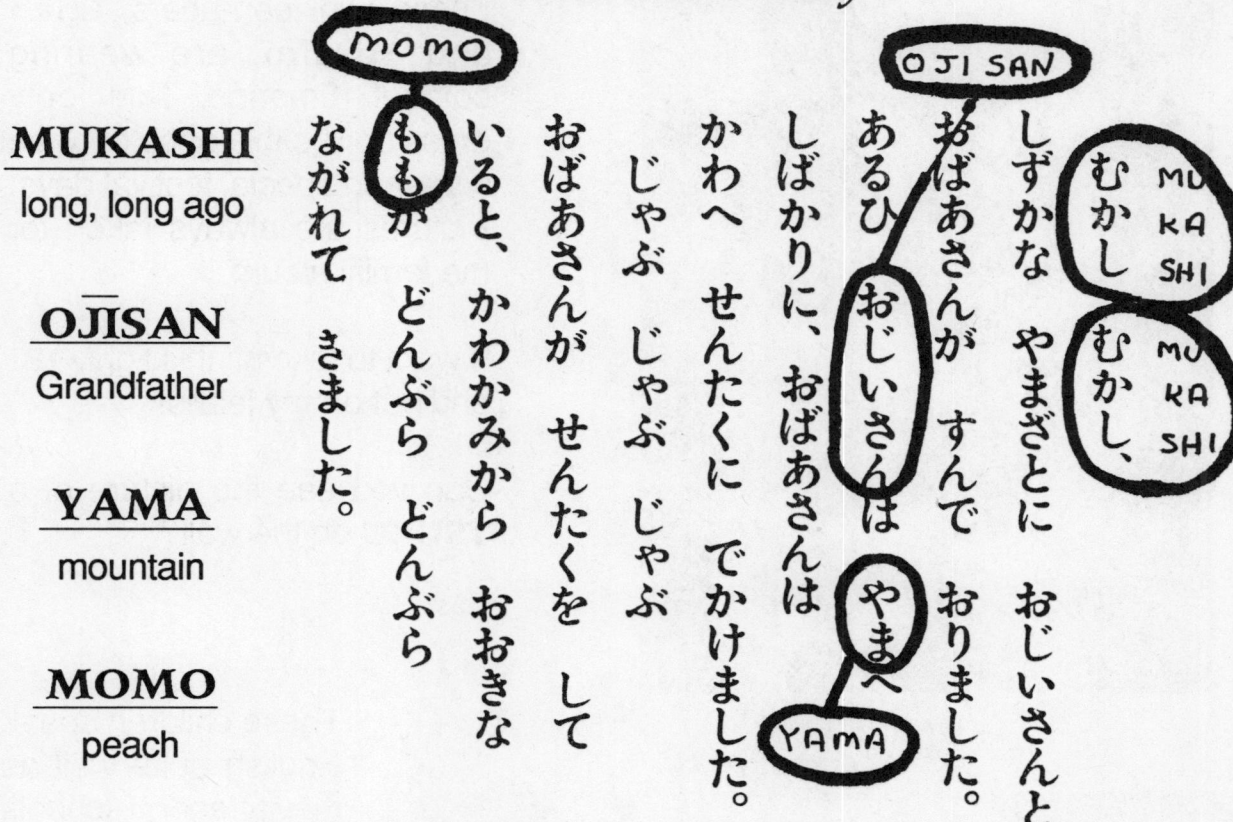

MUKASHI
long, long ago

OJĪSAN
Grandfather

YAMA
mountain

MOMO
peach

しずかな やまざとに おじいさんと おばあさんが すんで おりました。 あるひ、おじいさんは やまへ しばかりに、おばあさんは かわへ せんたくに でかけました。 じゃぶ じゃぶ じゃぶ おばあさんが せんたくを して いると、 かわかみから おおきな ももが どんぶら どんぶら ながれて きました。

むかし むかし (MUKASHI MUKASHI)
おじいさん (OJISAN)
やま (YAMA)
もも (MOMO)

Remember: Top to bottom, right to left
Can you find these words in the story above?

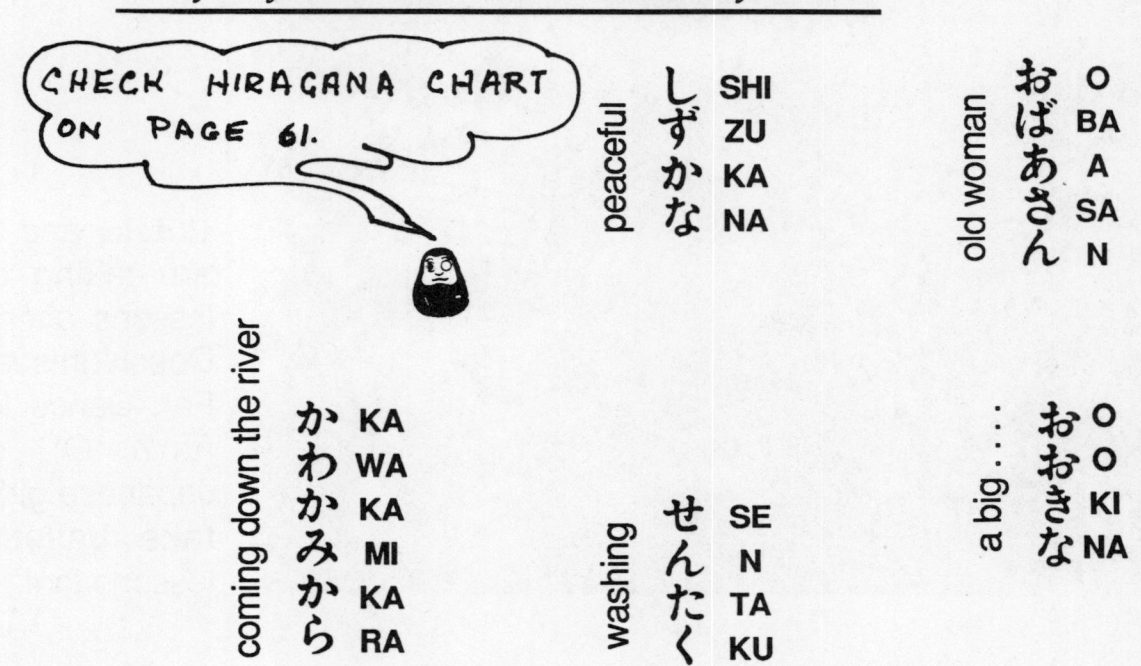

CHECK HIRAGANA CHART ON PAGE 61.

おばあさん O BA A SAN — old woman

おおきな O O KI NA — a big....

しずかな SHI ZU KA NA — peaceful

せんたく SE N TA KU — washing

かわかみから KA WA KA MI KA RA — coming down the river

65

These two teen-agers, **Eriko** and **Misako**, are wearing colorful Kimonos. They only dress up like this once or twice a year on special festival days. Pictures are always taken for the family album.

"I want to take off this tight **OBI** and put on my jeans!"

Can you see the picture of a **TSURU** on the wall?

These children speak English quite well as they attended schools in Bellevue for a few years.

Chiaki and **Mariko** are taking dancing lessons after school. Doesn't this Japanese Fan Dance look like fun? Of course, Japanese girls like to take ballet dance lessons too!

Chapter 7

The Japanese Home

At home . . . in Japan – Do I always have to take off my shoes?

KOTATSU – Can I hide under it?

Bedroom and Living Room – Two rooms in one!

Bathroom – I can't use soap?

Kitchen – No dishwasher? How can I exist!

Japanese Food – Breakfast – Lunch – Dinner.

Cook Rice Japanese style.

OYAKO DONBURI Recipe – 'Parent – child' dish.

SUSHI or **OSUSHI**

The family

Students and school

HARU'S **SEIJINSHIKI**

日本の家

NI HON NO IE

JAPAN A HOUSE

This is how I drink soup in Japan!

AT HOME... IN JAPAN

(oo–chee)
UCHI
house

(ee–eh)
IE
home

Many homes in Japan are half-Western and half-Japanese in design. The floors in the Japanese rooms are covered with **TATAMI** *(tah–tah–mee)* straw mats about four by six feet in size, and three inches thick. The **TATAMI** is clean because shoes are always removed at the front door. When you go to Japan remember to take your shoes off before you enter a home ... you will be given a pair of **SURIPPA** *(soo–ree–pah)* - slippers to wear inside.

The carpeted rooms have small tables and chairs, but sitting on the **TATAMI** is still preferred by most Japanese. It is comfortable on a big, flat **ZABUTON** *(zah–boo–tohn)* cushion with your legs stretched out under the **TSUKUE** *(tsoo–koo–eh)* table. Or you can sit on your legs the way the Japanese do ... but don't be surprised if after a few minutes they may be aching! Japanese love to rest in the **TATAMI** room, sip a cup of hot **OCHA** *(oh–cha)* tea at a low table, then get into a hot tub, **OFURO** *(oh–foo–roh)* bath and soak!

Remember the "U" sound is pronounced like "oo" in zoo.

ZABUTON
cushion

TSUKUE
desk

FURO
OFURO
bath

KOTATSU

KOTATSU (*koh–tah–tsoo*) Many homes in Japan have a **KOTATSU**. As there is no central heating in most houses, each room is heated separately with electricity. Some low tables have small built-in heating units underneath the top. In cold weather, a special blanket, or **FUTON** (*foo–tohn*), is put over the table-top, the extension cord is plugged in, and the **TSUKUE** low table becomes a nice, warm **KOTATSU**! Children do their homework, watch TV, play games or just talk . . . sitting around the **KOTATSU**.

Some homes have electrically heated carpets, too, that can be 'plugged in' during the cold weather. ***Remember, the Japanese always take off their shoes before entering a house.***

When you take off your shoes just inside the front door — there will be a pair of slip-on slippers 'waiting' for you!

Little children love to hide in the warm, dark 'secret' place under the **KOTATSU**.

THE BEDROOM & THE LIVING ROOM

(heh) (yah)
HE YA
部 屋

HEYA – ROOM

Japanese usually sleep right on the **TATAMI** straw mat floor, with a thick **FUTON** *(foo-tohn)* padded quilt underneath them, and another one on top. (Of course beds are used in hotels and homes where Westerners reside!) In the morning the **FUTONS** are folded and put on shelves behind sliding doors. Presto, like magic, a bedroom becomes a living room! And no beds to make! Does that sound like a good idea to you? It has always been done that way because Japanese homes are very small, and the rooms are used for many different activities. The islands of Japan are overcrowded, and the population is large. You seldom see big yards and 'sprawling' houses like we have in the US.

70

THE BATH ROOM

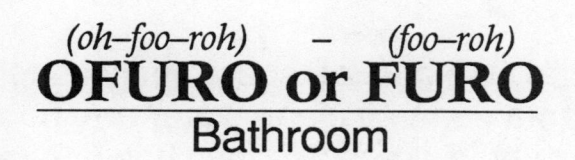

(oh–foo–roh) – *(foo–roh)*
OFURO or FURO
Bathroom

(bah soo)
BASSU
This is how the Japanese say our word BATH!

What is wrong with this picture? Is the water tap in the wrong place? Does it look like the water will run all over the floor? **No, nothing is wrong!** (The tap can be turned so that the water can go into the tub, or onto the tiled floor!)

This is the picture of a Japanese boy taking a **FURO**, or bath. In Japan a bathroom is really a BATH room! The tiled-floor room has only a bathtub; no toilet . . . no basin. The toilet and basin are in the small adjoining rooms.

If you visit a Japanese home and your friend asks "Would you like to have a nice, hot bath?" this is what you should do. Take off your clothes in the small 'dressing' room adjoining the bath. Then open the sliding door into the steamy, hot room. You will see that the tub is already full of water, almost to the top! (A heater in the side of the tub has heated the water.)

BATHROOM cont'

Before you get into the tub use the little bucket, soap, and washcloth to scrub your body. Then fill up the container with clean water and pour it all over yourself! What fun! Maybe you would like to use the shower? Yes, the floor will get wet, but if you look carefully you will see a drain in the floor. ***NEVER put soap into the bath. That is a NO NO!***

Only after you are washed and well rinsed is it time to get into the tub of steaming, hot water. Check it first! It may be too hot for you! If you are an adult you can sit on the bottom, and the water will come up to your chin! If you are a child, you will have to kneel! The water is clean, so the whole family can take turns in the same hot tub! Someone else will probably be waiting to get in as soon as you get out. In the USA we take a bath to wash ourselves, but in Japan a hot bath is enjoyed for soaking, and relaxing . . . especially after a long day at work or school! Does this little bathroom sound like fun to you?

• • • • • • • • • • • • • • • • • • •

The toilet in Japan is called **TOIRE** *(toh ee reh)*. If you ask, "Where is the bathroom?" you might not find what you are looking for! Just say **"Toire wa doko desu ka?"** or "Where is the **TOIRE**?"

72

KITCHEN

(dah–ee–doh–koh–roh)
DAIDOKORO

Japanese homes are full of modern-day conveniences, like computers, videos, stereos, microwave ovens, rice cookers, toasters, bread-makers, etc. but usually on a smaller scale. To us the tables and chairs look almost like children's furniture! Seldom do you see clothes dryers, large freezers for food. Washing machines are small, and most clothes are dried outside in the sunshine. Many apartments and homes have little porches where **FUTONS** may be aired.

Mothers go grocery shopping every day, so their food is always fresh. There are many small food shops all over Japan. Some just sell fish, others sell vegetables and some sell only baked goods. Fresh food in small quantities is preferred to frozen bulk foods. Large warehouse discount food stores are seldom seen in Japan. Where would the Japanese **OKĀSAN** *(oh–kāh–sahn)* mother store big bags of sugar, flour, potatoes, and oranges like your mother sometimes buys?

DAI 台

DOKORO 所

KITCHEN

A dishwasher in Japan is a rarity. Japanese kitchens are small – and the dishes are dainty. They must be washed by hand. A dishwasher would be more of a nuisance than a help! Believe it or not – dish dryers are becoming popular! Japan has a very humid climate!

JAPANESE FOOD ... TABEMONO
(tah–beh–moh–noh)

Do Japanese people eat a lot of rice? **Yes, they do!** Maybe **three times a day!** It is usually served plain, and dry ... never with gravy, milk, butter, or in rice pudding with cinnamon and raisins! **That sounds 'yucky' to them!** In recent years more bread or toast *(toh–soo–toh)* is being eaten for breakfast, and noodles for lunch. Now fast-foods like hamburgers and fried chicken have become favorites, Yes ... even tacos!

BREAKFAST ... ASAGOHAN
(ah–sah–goh–han)

GOHAN *(goh–han)* plain boiled rice, MISOSHIRU *(mee–soh–shee–roo)* soy bean paste soup, maybe some broiled fish, a raw or cooked egg, a small vegetable salad, some pickles, toast *(toh–soo–toh)* and coffee, or maybe tea, would be a quick simple breakfast before dashing off to the train station.

LUNCH ... HIRUGOHAN
(hee–roo–goh–hahn)

SOBA *(soh–bah)* (buckwheat noodles) or UDON *(oo–dohn)* (wheat noodles) with chicken, beef or fish on top. Boiled rice, cooked vegetables, TOFU *(toh–foo)* (bean curd), maybe some dried fish flakes or KAMABOKO *(kah–mah–boh–koh)* (fish cake). Pickles made out of long, white radishes, DAIKON *(dah–ee–kohn)* are a must. How about some SUSHI *(soo–shee)*, also called OSUSHI, maybe a delicious bowl of OYAKO DONBURI *(oh–yah–koh–dohn–boo–ree)*?
RECIPES AHEAD!
pg. 77

JAPANESE FOOD cont'

DINNER or SUPPER...YŪHAN

Yes, plain, boiled rice again! **MISO** *(mee-soh)* or a clear soup. Maybe some **SASHIMI** *(sah-shee-mee)* (raw fish), **YAKIMONO** *(yah-kee-moh-noh)* (grilled fish), **SUKIYAKI** *(soo-kee-yah-kee)* (sliced beef and vegetables prepared in a skillet), **TEMPURA** *(tehn-poo-rah)* (fish and vegetables prepared in a batter and then deep fried), **TOFU** *(toh-foo)* (soy bean curd). Desserts are seldom served. They are simple, like fresh fruit, or a plain sponge cake called **KASTERA** *(kahs-teh-rah)*, or maybe something made with **KANTEN** *(kahn-tehn)*. Kanten is a tasteless and colorless substance, made from seaweed and used like we use gelatin to "jell" liquid!

In most restaurants (except traditional Japanese) chairs and tables are used, but in the home, **IE**, *(ee-eh)*, sitting on the **TATAMI** *(tah-tah-mee)* around the low **TSUKUE** *(tsoo-koo-eh)* is still preferred. Food is attractively served on small, colorful dishes of different sizes and shapes. It is sometimes said that the Japanese "eat with their eyes" as well as their mouths. **HASHI** *(hah-shee)* (chopsticks) only are used for Japanese food. You had better practice before you go to Japan!

COOK RICE... Japanese Style

(go–hahn)
GOHAN 米

(for 3 people)
(Rice cooks better in larger quantities, so maybe you would like to double or triple the recipe.)

(koh–meh)
KOME

2 cups white rice (Japanese rice)
2 3/4 cups cold water (for dryer rice use 2 1/2 c water).

Measure out the rice and put it in a pan with cold water to cover. With your fingers swish it back and forth, then carefully drain off the milky liquid. Do this at least three or four times until the water becomes clear! Did you know that the Japanese washed their rice? Some housewives in Japan wash rice eight or ten times, and then let it rest in cold water for at least a half hour before cooking! This is the Japanese way!

Put the washed drained rice into a 2-3 quart pan with a tight lid, and add 2 3/4 cups of cold water. Cover with a tight lid, and turn the burner on high. Cook to a rapid boil, until it seems like the lid will POP OFF! Don't take the lid off, but turn down the heat as low as possible. Remember... don't stir and don't peek! In 15 minutes you will have some delicious, hot, 'sticky' **GOHAN** – rice... Japanese style. Turn heat off and let stand 10 minutes before serving. Of course, an automatic rice-cooker eliminates all this work! Now you can eat the rice plain, or with some shredded seaweed or powdered fish, and always with a pickle or two! Maybe you'd like to make **SUSHI** p. 78, or maybe **OYAKO DONBURI**, p. 77.

(oh–yah–koh   dohn–boo–ree)
OYAKO DONBURI

OYA means PARENT!   KO means CHILD!

Can you guess what it is? Of course, Chicken and Egg! *CHICKEN AND EGG DISH* recipe for 4. Maybe you will like it so well that this recipe will only be enough for two.

- 2 chicken breasts, boned and skinned
- 1 onion, sliced
- 3 **SHIITAKE** mushrooms sliced (any mushroom is ok, the more the better)
- 4 eggs– beaten slightly with a fork

Sauce:
- 1/4 cup water
- 4 Tbsp soy sauce (**OSHOYU**)
- 2 Tbsp sugar or **MIRIN** a sweet wine used in cooking.
- 1 tsp salt

Cut chicken in thin slices. Mix sauce and bring to a simmer in a skillet. Add chicken and cook 2 or 3 minutes until done. Add onions and mushrooms, cook for 1 minute. Beat eggs with a fork and slowly pour over the chicken. Cover and let cook until eggs are firm, about 1 minute. That's all! Isn't that easy? Then put one cup of cooked rice into a cereal bowl, a bowl for each person. Carefully scoop some of the chicken-vegetable mixture on top of the rice, and top with a few tablespoons of the delicious simmering sauce! Sliced green onions on top add to the flavor! Use chopsticks!

TANIN DONBURI or *"stranger in a bowl"* is when pork is used instead of chicken!

ITOKO DONBURI or *"cousin in a bowl"* is when beef is subsituted for chicken! And of course. . .

OYAKO DONBURI is *"parent and child"* bowl!

77

SU　す
SHI　し

SUSHI or OSUSHI

Some people in the US think **SUSHI** is "raw fish". This is wrong! **SUSHI** is a 'seasoned' rice . . . and only sometimes served with **SASHIMI** – raw fish on top. A favorite in Japan.

OSUSHI or **SUSHI** is a favorite Japanese dish food that has become a popular 'finger' food in the US during the past few years. The basic **SUSHI** rice is made with cooked white rice and flavored with a vinegar syrup.

For **SUSHI RICE** you need 5 cups of cooked rice and 3/4 cup syrup. **To make vinegar syrup**: 1/2 cup sugar, 3/4 cup rice vinegar, and 1 tablespoon salt. Bring to a boil and then cool. Sprinkle syrup over the cooked rice, mixing carefully not to mash the rice. Now you can make all sorts of **SUSHI**! In Japanese grocery stores in the U.S. you can buy bottles of 'ready mix' sushi syrup. This is easy to use and the flavor is always perfect!

SU
SHI

MAKI SUSHI is a **SUSHI** roll with **NORI** *(noh–ree)* sheets of seaweed on the outside and different ingredients on the inside. On a *'special'* bamboo matchstick mat, used only for rolling **SUSHI**, place a sheet of **NORI**. Spread seasoned rice about 1/2" thick on top of **NORI**. Place strips of *'various'* foods (maybe slices of seasoned omelette, mushrooms, fish, pickles, vegetables, etc.) along one edge, and roll up like a jellyroll. Cut into 1/2 to 3/4 inch slices.

SUSHI cont.

CALIFORNIA SUSHI

A *'modern'* SUSHI, probably invented in California, because it is made with avocados! It is also a rolled SUSHI, but the seaweed sheet is rolled on the inside. The outside is covered with sesame seeds GOMA *(goh-mah)*. In the center are thin slices of avocado.

(nee-gee-ree zoo-shee)
NIGIRIZUSHI

In this recipe the same seasoned SUSHI rice is pressed into small, deep fried bean cake bags, called AGE *(ah-geh)* or INARIZUSHI NO MOTO. These can be bought in a Japanese grocery store in cans or in the freezer section. Sometimes this SUSHI is tied with small pieces of NORI – seaweed.

(ee-nah-ree-zoo-shee)
INARIZUSHI

Is a favorite in Japan. It always has raw seafood or fish eggs on top! Using the palms of the hands, about 1/2 cup of SUSHI RICE is pressed into an oblong shaped rice ball and brushed with WASABI *(wah-sah-bee)* (horseradish paste). It is then topped with a thin slice of SASHIMI *(sah-shee-mee)*, (raw fish). It could be shrimp, tuna, squid, octopus, abalone, salmon, salmon eggs, geoduck, or any other fresh sea food. Even raw sea urchin is used. You must be careful where you buy NIGIRIZUSHI in the US. Go to a Japanese restaurant or a SUSHI bar where the fish is fresh. Thin slices of pink, pickled ginger and a small serving of light green WASABI are always served with OSUSHI . . . just like a hot dog is not a hot dog without yellow mustard!

(kah–zoh–koo)

KAZOKU
THE FAMILY

家族　KA ZOKU

OTŌSAN	*(oh–tōh–sahn)*	FATHER
OKĀSAN	*(oh–kāh–sahn)*	MOTHER
OBĀSAN	*(oh–bāh–sahn)*	GRANDMOTHER
OJĪSAN	*(oh–jēe–sahn)*	GRANDFATHER
ONĪSAN	*(oh–nēe–sahn)*	OLDER BROTHER
OTŌTO	*(oh–tōh–toh)*	YOUNGER BROTHER
ONĒSAN	*(oh–nēh–sahn)*	OLDER SISTER
IMŌTO	*(ee–mōh–toh)*	YOUNGER SISTER
AKAMBO	*(ah–kahm–boh)*	BABY, INFANT
O BASAN	*(oh–bah–sahn)*	AUNT
OJISAN	*(oh–jee–sahn)*	UNCLE

(The long sound is very important, as shown by the ——— over the vowels.)

Can you see the difference between AUNT and GRANDMA, and between UNCLE and GRANDPA?

(gahk–koh)
GAKKŌ
SCHOOL

GAKUSEI	*(gahk–seh–ee)*	STUDENT
SENSEI	*(sehn–seh–ee)*	TEACHER
SHŌGAKKŌ	*(sho–gahk–kōh)*	ELEMENTARY SCHOOL
CHŪGAKKŌ	*(choo–gahk–kōh)*	MIDDLE SCHOOL
KŌTŌGAKKŌ	*(koh–toh–gahk–kōh)*	HIGH SCHOOL

Most students in middle school and high school wear a uniform. The other requirements are **no** lipstick, **no** earrings, **no** jewelry, **no** make-up, skirts must be a certain length. The shoes, socks and school bags are also the school's decision! **Absolutely NO curly hair!**

GAKKŌ NO NAMAE WA NAN DESU KA?
What's the name of your school?

TAKOMA CHŪGAKKŌ DESU.
It's Tacoma Middle School.

(sehn–seh–ee noh nah-mah-eh wah nahn dehss kah)
SENSEI NO NAMAE WA NAN DESU KA?
What's your teacher's name?

SUMISU SENSEI DESU
It's Mr. Smith

81

SEI JIN SHIKI

January 15 – 20 Years Old
"MATURE PERSON CEREMONY"

In this picture HARU is wearing a beautiful long-sleeved kimono for SEIJINSHIKI.

On January 15, 20-year old men and women attend public meetings held by local officials in city auditoriums. They listen to speeches of congratulations and advice on entering the adult world! Sometimes the speeches are boring, but the students love to get together and see old friends. Its almost like a school reunion! They dress up in their best clothes – traditional Japanese or Western.

HARU is wearing a kimono given to her by her grandfather. Lots of pictures are taken on this special day. HARU may wear this kimono again on a special occasion – or she may save it for her own wedding and wear it as an extra kimono. After that the long sleeves must be cut. Only single girls may wear long sleeved Kimonos. HARU will probably put hers in a box and save it for her future family.

"This is how I looked when I was 20!"

HARU graduated from Bellevue High School with honors – and is presently an architect in OSAKA.

Chapter 8

Festivals... Special Days... and "Things"

FESTIVAL

祭

MATSURI

New Year's Festival... **OSHŌ GATSU** 1/1, **MOCHI, HAGOITA** and kites.

SETSUBUN... Bean Throwing Day 2/3, **DARUMA**

OHINA MATSURI... Girl's Day or Doll Festival 3/3

TANGO NO SEKKU... Boy's Day 5/5

TANABATA 7/7,...**BON ODORI**

JŪGOYA... Moon Viewing 9/15, Tooth Fairy, **KENDAMA** Game.

SHICHI–GO–SAN (7-5-3) Festival 11/15

Wedding Picture

Where is number 4?

Is Number 4 unlucky? **IKEBANA**.

いろいろな事 — I RO I RO NA KOTO — **DIFFERENT THINGS**

Can you find the number 4 on this page?

(ee–roh ee–roh)
IRO IRO
DIFFERENT

(nah koh–toh)
NA KOTO
THINGS

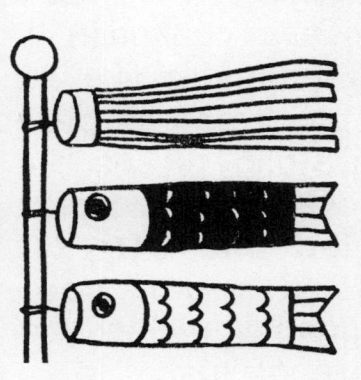

HAPPY NEW YEAR

SHŌ GATSU

正月

(oh–shōh gah–tsoo
OSHO GATSU
THE NEW YEAR

(sheen–nehn oh–meh–deh–tōh)
SHINNEN OMEDETO
HAPPY NEW YEAR

A decoration for the New Year is prepared in the home — two, big, flattened balls of **MOCHI** *(moh chee)* or rice balls, and always with a **MIKAN** *(mee kahn)* tangerine on top. (Sometimes the word **OMOCHI** is used. Adding an "o" makes a word *honorable* or more *polite*!) These two balls are placed in a prominent place, like we display a Christmas tree! Later in the month this **MOCHI** is eaten. It is so much fun to cut the big ball into pieces and eat it with the whole family!

MOCHI or OMOCHI

This delicious food is made by cooking a *sweet mochi rice* until it is very soft. It is then pounded with a big mallet and pressed into cakes. Some are flat and rectangular. Others are big and round, and prepared especially for the New Year. **MOCHI** may be served in soup, or cooked in the oven until it puffs up like a marshmallow. It can be pulled into long, stringy pieces, like string cheese! Then it tastes good dipped into **SHOYU** (soy sauce) sugar sauce or wrapped with small pieces of seaweed! Yum! And so much fun to eat!

MAY I HAVE SOME, PLEASE

MAY I HELP YOU CUT THE MOCHI

84

SHIN NEN OMEDETŌ – Happy New Year cont'

Sometimes the little girls play a game with a **HAGOITA** *(hah-go-ee-tah)* battledore, and a feathered **HANE** *(hah-neh)* . . . like a badminton "birdie". One side of the wooden **HAGOITA** is flat like a paddle. On the other side, made out of padded material, is the face of a beautiful woman. Even the hair feels like real hair, so soft and silky! This game is played along the side of the street. No net is needed!

Boys often fly kites, **TAKO** *(tah-koh)*. Some of them have brightly painted faces on them, of ancient warriors and **SAMURAI** *(sah-moo-rah-ee)*. They look so colorful against the blue sky.

HAGOITA

HANE

85

(seh tsoo boo n)

SETSUBUN
BEAN THROWING DAY
February 3

On this day children and adults throw roasted soy beans outside! If you listen closely you may hear them saying... **"ONI WA SOTO"**... or "out with the devil and bad things" *(oh–nee–wah soh–toh)*! Inside the house more beans are being tossed around! **"FUKU WA UCHI"** *(foo–koo wah oo–chee)*, "may good things and happiness be in our home"! Sometimes candy and gum are thrown in the air along with the beans! Then it is fun to gather up all the 'goodies', and eat them! Often the children wear funny masks that have ugly faces like an ogre or an **ONI** *(oh–nee)* – a devil with horns! Doesn't this sound like a fun festival?

(dah–roo–mah)
DARUMA

A **DARUMA** doll can be found in a Japanese novelty store, or in little shops near famous shrines. These ball-like dolls have rounded bottoms. They used to be made out of clay or paper mache, but recently many are made out of plastic.

Sometimes a **DARUMA** is a *'tumbling doll'* because...

86

DARUMA cont'

when you hit it, it always comes back to the same position! It is weighted in the bottom! This doll means GOOD LUCK! It is red all over, except for the face which has two big round eyes.

Some **DARUMA** are very small, no larger than your thumb, and others may be taller than you are! There are eyeless **DARUMA** too. The person who receives this as a gift, or buys one for himself, does it only for *"good luck"*. He paints one eye on the face. Only when the wish comes true, or Good Luck arrives, does the funny, round face get its second eye! Sometimes it may take one or two years. College students love to paint a second eye when they finally graduate!

Watch TV news the next time there is an election in Japan. The newly elected prime minister is often seen adding the missing eye to a DARUMA that is almost as big as he is!

DARUMA is named after **BODHIDHARMA**, an Indian Buddhist missionary in China over 1,300 years ago. He was the founding patriarch of ZEN Buddhism. It is said that he sat on a rock, high up in the mountains, and prayed . . . and prayed . . . and prayed for so many years that his legs disappeared! The stubby, round legless *'doll'* appears to have a loose coat covering his head, with only his face showing.

(oh–hee–nah mah–tsoo–ree)
OHINA MATSURI
DOLL FESTIVAL . . . Girl's Day

March 3 . . . 3rd day of the 3rd month

Each home that has a daughter displays dolls, often a set of traditional dolls representing the Prince and Princess, their maids of honor, five musicians, two guardsmen and three footmen. The fifteen dolls are arranged on seven steps. On the bottom shelves are miniature pieces of furniture, carriages, tiny chests of drawers, soup bowls with lids, teensie-weensie shoes, bows and arrows, and musical instruments that even have strings!

It is a fairylands of dolls! **But . . . the dolls are only to look at, not to play with.** The Prince and Princess are always on the top shelf. Their clothes are made of beautiful silk brocade, and in very fine detail. The display may be set up in February, but on March 4 it is usually taken down. Everything is individually wrapped and carefully boxed until the next **HINAMATSURI** DAY.

OHIMESAMA IS THE WORD FOR PRINCESS

Ohina sama
O HI NA SAMA
is the word for doll

88

OHINA MATSURI cont'

There is a myth that if dolls are left on display too long, the daughter will be very old when she gets married! Sometimes the young girls appear in beautiful kimonos but sadly this custom is fast disappearing. A pretty Western style dress is more comfortable. A small child may wear a kimono, but only for a picture. The family album is very important!

Girls visit their friends to see their doll displays; drink a special non-alcoholic **SAKE** *(sah-keh)* or rice wine, eat **ARARE** *(ah-rah-reh)* or small grains of sugared-puffed rice in pretty spring colors . . . white, pink, and light green. **ARARE** is also the Japanese word for hail! Small white grains look like pieces of icy snow! Can you see the **SAKURA MOCHI** *(sah-koo-rah moh-chee)* on the table? **SAKURA** means cherry blossom. Small cubes of **MOCHI** are wrapped in cherry tree leaves to make this special treat. Peach blossoms, **MOMO** *(moh-moh)*, symbolize happiness in marriage.

These dolls are often handed down from grandmother to granddaughter, so some antique sets are very valuable. Girls may also display other favorite dolls, dolls they can *play* with, but the **HINA MATSURI** dolls are just to look at and admire!

(tahn–goh noh sehk–koo)

TANGO NO SEKKU

BOY'S DAY

also called

(koh–doh–moh noh hee)

KODOMO–NO–HI
CHILDREN'S DAY

May 5 . . . fifth day of the fifth month

On Boy's Day, **TANGO**, parents display colorful fish-like wind socks from high flag poles. The carp, **KOI** *(koh ee)*, is a strong fish, and can overcome problems. The parents hope their sons will grow up to be manly, honest, brave, and be able to cope with problems, just like the strong **KOI**.

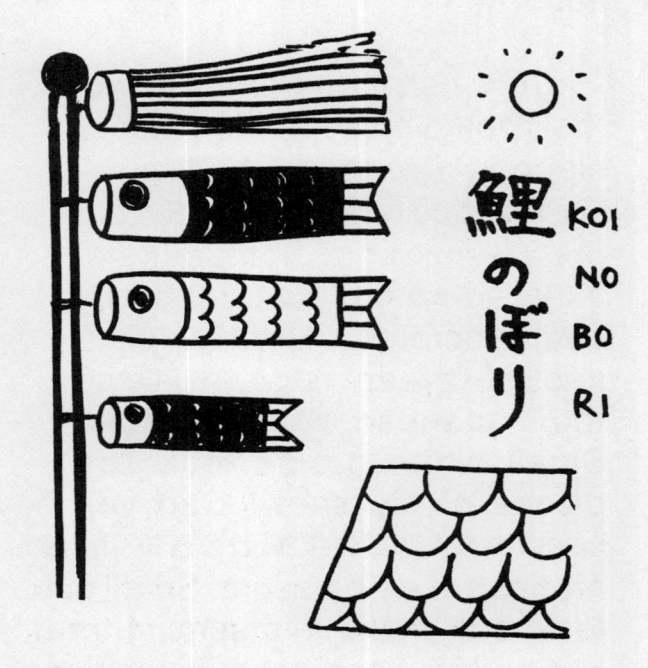

鯉のぼり KOI NO BO RI

The big fish on the top is for daddy, and it is black or blue. The next one is red and it is for mother. Each son in the family has a blue fish. These fish are flown only around BOY'S DAY, for a few weeks . . . not during the rest of the year, as you sometimes see in the US!

How many fish can you count from this train window?

(Photo courtesy of Japan National Tourist Organization.)

TANGO NO SEKKU cont'

(kah–boo–toh)
KABUTO
HELMET

While the **KOI** *(koh–ee)* are flying in the wind outside, male dolls dressed in costumes of ancient warriors are displayed on a special shelf inside the house. There are also miniature suits of armor, helmets, bows and arrows, and **TANGO** festive foods. Everything has a special meaning, and symbolizes honesty and strength as seen in the warriors and **SAMURAI** of ancient Japan. The iris, **SHOBU** *(shoh boo)*, is the **TANGO** flower. It is *royal* purple in color, and the leaves are long and sharp like swords!

A "boy" doll for Boy's Day.

A special food for **TANGO** is **CHIMAKI** *(chee mah kee)*. Cooked rice is wrapped in a long, slim bamboo leaf, and steamed. **KASHIWA MOCHI** *(kah shee wah)* is a rice cake with sweetened bean paste inside, wrapped in an oak leaf, and steamed.

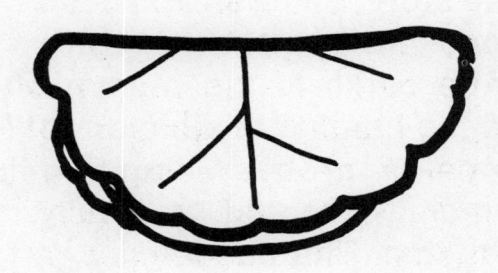

(tah–nah–bah–tah)

TANABATA

JULY 7

7th day of the 7th month.

Seventh day of the seventh month. This is a fun day! Children write their own wishes and poems on little strips of paper and hang them on a bamboo branch! It looks almost like a decorated Christmas tree! If there are no bamboo trees in your neighborhood, you can always buy a branch at the store. On this special night the Milky Way is said to become clearly visible!

I hope my wish comes true!

(bohn oh–doh–ree)

BON ODORI

JULY 15

"Welcoming Home"
Dance for the Spirits

The **BON ODORI** festival welcomes back to earth the spirits of those who have died! This is an old Japanese story. Children and adults love to dance the **OBON** *(oh bohn)* in the shrine parks to the rhythm of music and the beating of a big drum! People dance in groups, clapping hands, stamping feet and gracefully moving in rhythm. The dance may go far into the night. In olden days, sometimes even until dawn!

Let's dance all night!

(joo–goh–yah)
JUGOYA
MOON VIEWING
SEPTEMBER 15

The moon is big, and full and round! What fun it is to eat **ODANGO** *(oh dahn goh)*, dumplings that mother has prepared especially for this night! The whole family enjoys the cool, evening air while watching the big moon move slowly across the sky. Doesn't that sound like fun? Do you think bedtime is a little later than usual on **JUGOYA**?

THE TOOTH FAIRY

Is there a TOOTH FAIRY in Japan? Well, not exactly a fairy, but Japanese children believe that if they throw their lower baby teeth up on the roof, and their upper baby teeth down under the house, their new teeth will grow to be strong and healthy! Maybe a Tooth Fairy can do that?

(kehn–dah–man)
KENDAMA

In this fun game a small wooden ball is attached by a string to a wooden *hammer*. Hold the handle with one hand, and with a lifting motion try to rest the ball in one of the three (1, 2, 3) *cups* or on the *peg*. The (4) *peg* is the most difficult!

93

SHICHI – GO – SAN
SEVEN-FIVE-THREE FESTIVAL
November 15
We would say 'Three-Five-Seven', wouldn't we?

This very special day is only for **little boys, aged five**, and **little girls, aged three and seven**! Children in Japan dress in Western-style clothes, and in school wear a uniform; but on **SHICHI-GO-SAN** day colorful kimonos appear on the little girls. The tinier the girl, the more brilliantly she is dressed. Sometimes the five year old boy wears a **HAKAMA** *(hah–kah–mah)*. It is a long pleated skirt . . . a carryover from ancient days. Often a **HAORI** *(hah-o-ree)* or short kimono-type coat is worn over the **HAKAMA**. Parents, grandparents and children aged '3–5–7' go to nearby shrines. There they offer blessings and thanks for good health and happiness. It is fun to parade their fashions around the shrine parks!

Children receive **CHITOSE** *(chee–toh–seh)* candy – a pair of red and white stick candy about fifteen inches long. It always comes in a very special bag with a handle. **CHITOSE** candy is as exciting to Japanese children as Christmas candy canes are to American children. Family pictures are taken on this important day.

If you have any Japanese friends ask them to show you their **SHICHI-GO-SAN** pictures! I'm sure they will have some! It may be the only time they have worn a **HAKAMA** or a bright, colorful **KIMONO** and **OBI** *(oh bee)* – a wide sash tied into a big bow. Sometimes it looks like a colorful butterfly on the back of the **KIMONO**! Can you see the **KANJI** on their bags? ***"May you have 1,000 years of happiness."*** The KANJI for 1,000 is 千   七 五 三

KEKKON NO SHASHIN – A WEDDING PICTURE

kehk kohn   noh   shah sheen
KEKKON NO SHASHIN
WEDDING PICTURE

This couple is dressed for a traditional Japanese wedding. The bride is wearing a beautiful **KIMONO** with long *'sleeves'* that reach to the floor! The ornate **OBI** is brocaded, often with gold threads running through it. She is wearing a wig, in an old fashioned hair style, decorated with flowers and ornaments. The groom is wearing a **HAORI** *(hah-oh-ree)* coat, and a **HAKAMA** *(hah-kah-mah)* – a long pleated skirt.

After a formal traditional ceremony and the all important *picture taking*, the couple will change into Western style wedding clothes . . . a long, formal white wedding gown, and a handsome tuxedo! More pictures will be taken for that very precious family album! Often there is a third change of clothes! This time the bride wears a shorter Western style dress. These clothes are usually rented.

A beautifully decorated wedding cake, maybe three or four feet high, will be on display. It is also rented. You can't eat it because it is probably made of cardboard – covered with icing! It is an imitation wedding cake!

Japanese weddings and banquets often last four or five hours – with speeches, toasts, and lots of special foods. No wedding gifts are given as in the US, but each guest leaves a small envelope with money for the new couple.

NUMBER 4

Is 4 a bad number? (Can you find the number 4 on the previous pages?) Are 1–3 – 5 –7 –11– 15 *good numbers*? **Never** are 4 cookies or 4 pieces of fruit served on a plate. Dishes come in sets of 5 – never 4 or 6.

(ee keh bah nah)
IKEBANA

This is the Japanese word for the art of flower arrangement. Look carefully . . . the flowers and branches are in odd numbers! The top branch or flower represents <u>heaven</u>, the next one is a <u>man</u>, and the lowest represents <u>earth</u>.

NUMBER 4

The number **4** is pronounced **shi**. **Shi** is also the word for ***death.*** Do you think that is the reason why **4** is considered an unlucky number? In hospitals and hotels there are no No. 4 rooms! Does this sound a little like our No. 13?

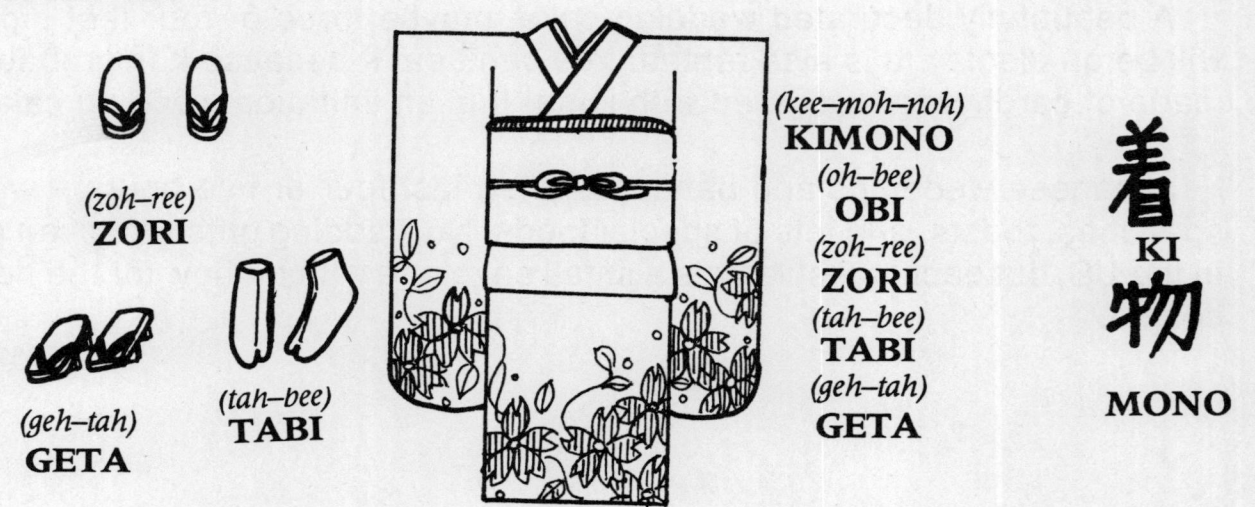

(zoh–ree) **ZORI**
(geh–tah) **GETA**
(tah–bee) **TABI**
(kee–moh–noh) **KIMONO**
(oh–bee) **OBI**
(zoh–ree) **ZORI**
(tah–bee) **TABI**
(geh–tah) **GETA**

KI
MONO

Chapter 9

STORIES, SONGS, ORIGAMI

CHILDREN'S STORIES
- MOMOTARŌ
- The Fairy Crane
- The Tongue-Cut Sparrow

CHILDREN'S SONGS
- The Rain Song
- Pigeon Song
- The Sun is Setting
- The Hare and the Tortoise
- Tulip Song
- Cherry Blossoms

FINGER SONG

TONGUE TWISTERS

ORIGAMI . . . Bird, Helmet, Balloon, Box

CRANE SENBA ZURU . . . 1,000 Cranes

(koh–doh–moh noh)
KO DO MO NO
こどもの
CHILDREN'S

(moh–noh)
MONO
THINGS

I AM A KODOMO

(gah–tah–ree)
GATARI
STORIES

(oo–tah)
UTA
SONGS

A YU MI NO NO RO I

(oh) **O**
(ree) **RI**
(gah) **GA**
(mee) **MI**

おりがみ

MOMOTARŌ
Little Peach Boy

ももたろう
MO　　MO　　TA　　RŌ

Once upon a time an old man and an old woman lived all alone in a small mountain village. One day the old man went into the woods to gather firewood, and the old woman went to the river to wash her clothes. **Suddenly she saw a very big peach floating down the river!** At first she couldn't believe her eyes! She decided to take it home. Her husband said, **"Quick! Let's cut it open!"** What do you think was inside? **Out jumped a little baby boy!**

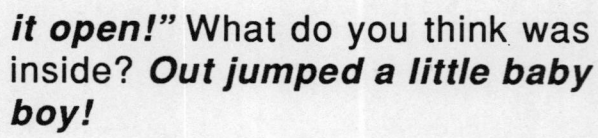

The old man and the old woman were so happy, and they decided to raise him as their son. No longer would they be lonesome. They named him **MOMOTARŌ**, or Peachboy. **MOMO** means *"peach"* in Japanese, and **TARŌ** is a common ending for a boy's name.

MOMOTARŌ cont'

MOMOTARŌ grew up to be a fine young man. One day he said to his parents, *"I am going to the Island of Giants and fight the wicked monsters who stole treasures from you and the other villagers."*

His mother gave him a small bag of wheat flour balls, **KIBIDANGO** *(kee-bee-dahn-goh)*, to eat on the way. A short distance down the road **MOMOTARO** met a dog, then a monkey, and later a pheasant.

"Will you come and help me fight the **ONI** *(monsters)?"* he asked his new friends.

"Will you share your **KIBI DANGO***?"* they asked **MOMOTARO**. Of course the answer was *"yes"*!

After a long hike and a boat ride, they finally arrived at the island. The **ONI** had seen them coming and were waiting on the beach. In the battle that followed the dog bit the monsters, the monkey scratched the **ONI** and the pheasant swooped down and stabbed them with his long, sharp beak! The brave **MOMOTARO** had a lot of help from is faithful friends. Finally, covered with cuts and bruises, the **ONI** gave up.

MOMOTARŌ cont'

"We are sorry. Please forgive us. We will never do it again. Here are all the treasures we stole. Please take them back to the villagers."

MOMOTARŌ and his three friends carried the treasures home to the happy villagers. They gave him a true hero's welcome.

"I couldn't have done it alone," he said. *"My dear friends . . . the dog, the monkey and the pheasant . . . all helped me. And thank you, mother, for the delicious KIBIDANGO!"*

SHITA KIRI SUZUME
THE TONGUE-CUT SPARROW

Once upon a time there lived an old man and an old woman. The old man had a pet sparrow which he loved very much. One day, after a long, hard hike through the woods he arrived home and immediately went to see his little bird. The cage was empty!

"Where is my little sparrow?" he asked his wife. At first she said she didn't know. *"You are lying. He would never fly away. I have been kind to him all his life, and love him very much."*

"Well, he is gone forever! He flew away! He ate some of my washing starch that I had put outside in a bowl. I was so angry, I cut off his tongue! He will NEVER do that again!"

"You are a wicked and unkind woman," he said. *"That poor little bird didn't hurt you at all. When you put food outside in a bowl it is always for the birds!"* Immediately the old man went out in search of his dear little friend.

"Where are you? Where are you, little Tongue-cut Sparrow?" he called out as he wandered through the woods.

The sparrow recognized his master's voice.

"Here I am! Here I am! Standing beside the bamboo grove. How kind of you to come looking for me. Please come to my house for some tea and refreshments. My family and I will dance for you. You are my very dear friend."

SHITA KIRI SUZUME cont'

The old man followed the Tongue-cut Sparrow into a lovely little house made of bamboo. The sparrows were dressed in colorful kimonos. After the Sparrow Dance the old man was served tea and cakes.

"It is getting dark. I must go home now," said the old man.

"Please come again," said the little Tongue-cut Sparrow. *"I have a present for you. Please choose. One is big and the other is small. You pick one."*

"Oh," said the old man, *"I am weak and old, and the walk home is long. I would like the smaller box. Thank you so very much, Tongue-cut Sparrow, you are so very kind,"* and he started down the dusty path.

"Please come in! We will dance for you, dear master!"

When he got home his wife was waiting at the door.

"Where have you been, and what's in the box? Open it, you old man!" and she grabbed it from her tired husband. When she took off the lid, for a minute here eyes were blinded by the bright jewels, gold and treasures. *"And you chose the smaller box? Are you out of your mind? I will visit the Sparrow House myself. Maybe they will give me the larger box!"*

Excitedly she started out in search of the bamboo grove and the little house.

SHITA KIRI SUZUME cont'

"Little Tongue-cut Sparrow! Little Tongue-cut Sparrow! Here I am . . . the wife of your kind master!"

Suddenly she saw the little sparrow dressed in a beautiful kimono.

"Would you like some tea, old woman?"

"I don't have much time. It is getting dark, but I can visit a few minutes."

After refreshments the sparrows asked her to choose a box. Of course, she chose the biggest one she saw.

"It is very large and heavy. Are you sure you want that one!"

"Oh, yes. I am younger and stronger than my old man. It is not too heavy for me!"

The greedy old woman grabbed the box and headed out the door. She couldn't wait until she got home, so she stopped a short distance down the path and took off the lid. What do you think was inside? Oh! out jumped lizards, out crawled snakes, out flew bugs and beetles, and inside sat some awful looking monsters . . . but no jewels, and no gold!

That is what the Tongue-cut Sparrow and his friends thought the nasty, old woman deserved. What do you think?

YŪ ZURU
THE FAIRY CRANE

夕鶴 YŪ ZURU

Once upon a time an old man and an old woman lived all alone in the country. They were very lonely because they didn't have any children. One day, when the old man was walking home with his bundle of fire wood he noticed the tall grasses moving along the side of the path. He looked closely and saw a big, white crane, twisting and turning in pain. It appeared to be trapped. The farmer felt so sorry for the beautiful bird. He carefully cut it loose and watched it fly into the blue sky. Then he hurried home and excitedly told his wife what had happened.

"It was as white as snow! I have never seen such a beautiful bird! As it flew away it seemed to flap its wings. I think was was saying 'thank you' to me!"

That evening there was a knock at the door. A pretty little girl was standing outside in the dark.

"I'm lost. May I spend the night with you?"

"Of course", they replied. *"But where did you come from, pretty girl?"*

She only smiled: *"Thank you for letting me stay with you. I don't have a home."*

104

YŪ ZURU cont'

They had a happy evening together sitting around the glowing **HIBACHI** *(hee–bah–chee)* *(a charcoal fire pot used for both cooking and heating)* and sipping **MISO** soup and tea.

"We wish you would stay with us. We are lonesome . . . just the two of us. We would love to have a daughter! Will you be part of our family?"

• • • • • • • • • • • • • •

One day the little girl said: *"I see you have a loom. I would like to weave something for you, but please promise that you will never peek into my room!"*

Where is my little girl?

Every night the little girl gave her new parents a beautiful piece of cloth. How could she weave so quickly? It was like a miracle! And the fabric seemed to shine and glisten like magic.

The old woman was bursting with curiosity. One day she decided to take just a little peek! No one would ever know! She slowly opened the sliding paper door.

Where was the little girl? She looked again . . . but all she saw was a beautiful white crane sitting in front of the loom, and spinning! It was using some of its own white feathers to weave the sparkling cloth! The old woman couldn't even tell her husband what she had seen, because she knew she had broken a promise.

YŪ ZURU cont'

That night the little girl said: *"Now you know my secret! Dear parents, I am the crane that was caught in the snare. You saved my life. I wanted to show my thanks. I was hoping I could stay with you for a long time. You have been so kind to me, and I love you very much. But now I can no longer stay with you. I must go back to where I came from."*

With tears in their eyes, the old man and the old woman waved goodbye as a big white crane flew into the sky, circled the house a few times and then slowly disappeared into the distance.

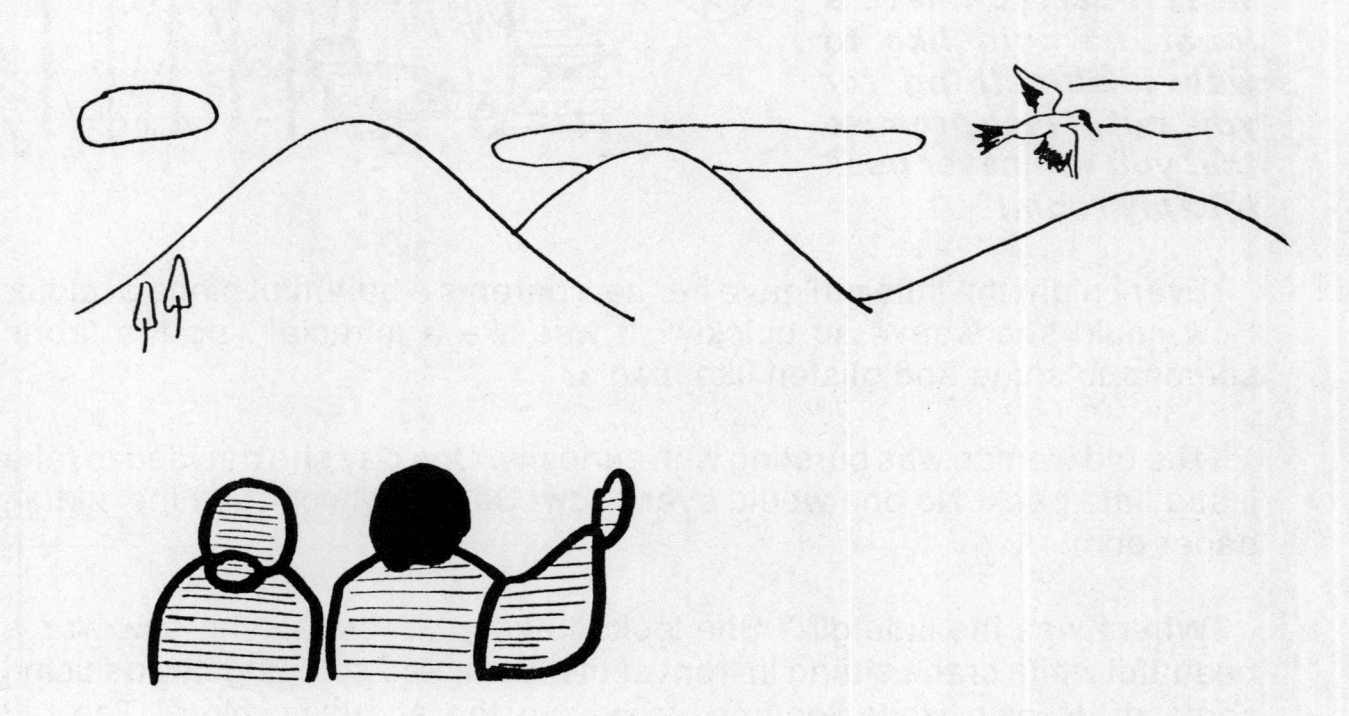

(ah meh   no   oo tah)
AME NO UTA
THE RAIN SONG

(ah–meh, ah–meh, foo–reh, foo–reh)
AME, AME, FURE, FURE.
It's raining, it's raining

(kah–ah–sahn gah)
KASAN GA,
mother is

(jah–noh–meh deh oh–moo–kah–eh)
*JANOME DE OMUKAE
picking me up – and she
has a big umbrella

(oo–reh–shee–ee nah)
URESHII NA
I'm so happy.

(pee–chee! pee–chee! chah–poo! chah–poo!)
PICHI! PICHI! CHAPU! CHAPU!
It's raining, it's raining

(rahn! rahn! rahn!)
RAN! RAN! RAN!
(These words are all rain sounds – like we say 'pitter patter'!)

*JANOME *is an old fashioned oiled paper, bamboo ribbed umbrella.* **KASA** *is the word for ☂ today.*

A ME A ME FU RE FU RE KA A SA N GA JA NO ME DE O MU KA E

U RE SHI I NA PI CHI PI CHI CHA PU CHA PU RAN RAN RAN

HATO NO UTA
PIGEON SONG

(poh poh poh hah–toh poh poh)
PO PO PO, HATO PO PO
(Po...po...po...little pigeons...

(mah meh gah hoh–she–e kah, soh–rah yah–roo zoh)
MAME GA HOSHII KA, SORA YARU ZO
Do you want some beans? I'll give you some, if you will

(meen–nah deh nah–kah yoh–koo tah–beh nee koh–ee)
MINNA DE NAKA YOKU, TABE NI KOI
be friendly to one another... and lets come and eat together.)

HATO
PIGEONS

MAME
BEANS

HOSHI
TO WANT

MINA
ALL

TABERU
TO EAT

PO PO PO HA TO PO PO MA ME GA HO SHI I KA SO RA YA RU ZO

MI NA DE NA KA YO KU TA BE NI KO I

THE SUN SETTING

(yoo yah–keh koh yah–keh deh, hee gah koo–reh–tah)
YU YAKE KO YAKE DE, HI GA KURETA,
The sun is setting

(yah–mah noh oh–teh–rah noh)
YAMA NO OTERA NO
The mountain temple

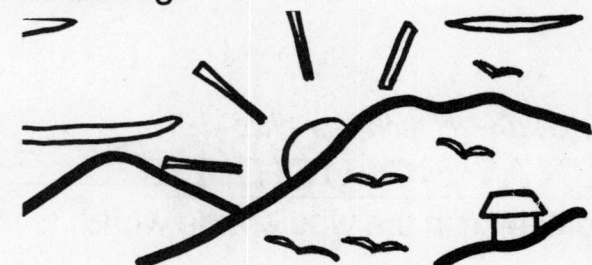

(kah–neh gah nah–roo)
KANE GA NARU
bell is ringing

(oh–teh–teh tsoo–nah–ee–deh mee–nah kah–eh–roh)
OTETE TSUNAIDE MINA KAERO
Let's hold hands and go home

(kah–rah–soo toh ee–shoh–nee kah–eh–ree mah–shoh)
KARASU TO ISSHONI KAERI MASHOO
along with the crows.

MOSHI MOSHI KAME YO
THE HARE AND TORTOISE SONG (Aesop's Fables)

(moh–shee moh–shee kah–meh yoh, kah–meh sahn yoh
MOSHI MOSHI KAME YO, KAME SAN YO
Hello! Hello! Mr. Tortoise

seh–kah–ee noh oo–chee–deh
SEKAI NO UCHI DE
No one else in the whole wide world

oh–mah–eh hoh–doh
OMAE HODO,
like you

ah–yoo–mee noh noh–roh–ee moh–noh wah nah–ee
AYUMI NO NOROI MONO WA NAI,
walks so slowly!

doh–shee–teh sohn nah–nee noh–roh–ee noh kah)
DOSHITE SON NANI NOROI NO KA.
I wonder why you are so slow.

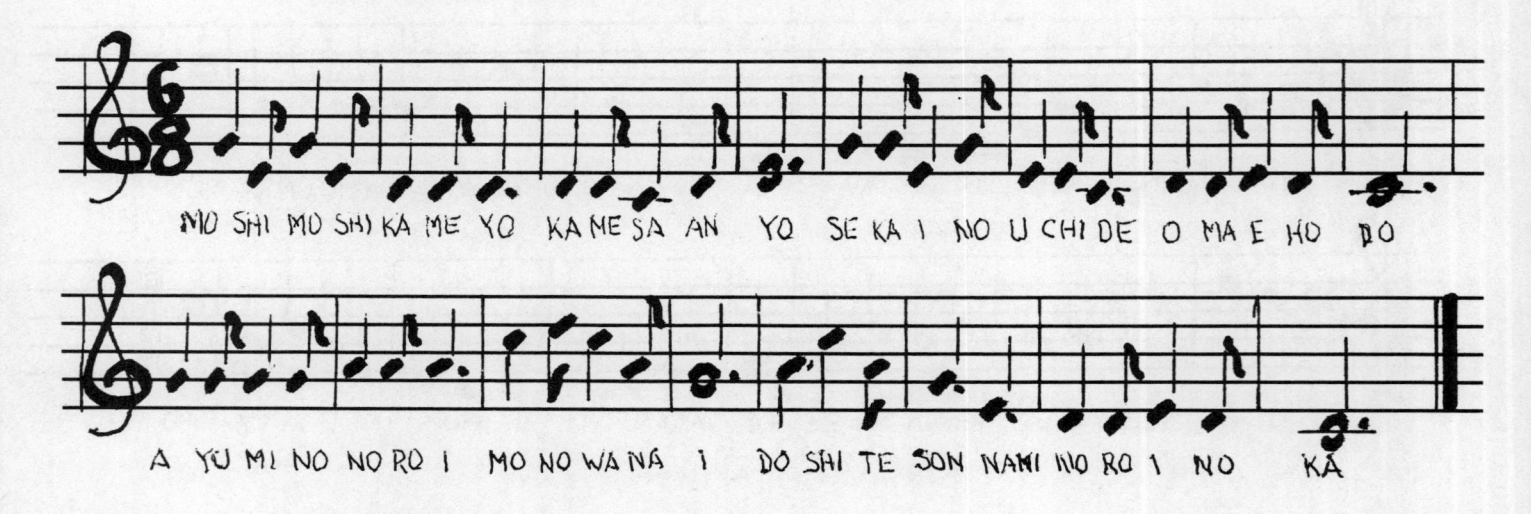

110

(chōo – ree – poo noh oo–tah)
CHURIPPU NO UTA
THE TULIP SONG

(sah–ee–tah, sah–ee–tah
SAITA, SAITA
Blooming, blooming

chōo–ree–poo noh hah–nah gah
CHURIPPU NO HANA GA,
The tulips are blooming

nah–rahn–dah, nah–rahn–dah
NARANDA, NARANDA,
Row on row, row on row

ah–kah, shee–roh, kee–ee–roh
AKA, SHIRO, KIIRO,
Red, white, yellow

doh–noh hah–nah mee–teh–moh
DONO HANA MITEMO,
wherever I look the flowers

kee–reh–ee dah nah)
KIREI DA NA.
are so pretty.

> A "chūrippu" is a tulip.
> Note: the 'ree' in Japanese sounds like a 'dee' to us.
> 'choo–ree–poo' sounds like 'choo–dee–poo'
> This overlapping sound of "d" and "r" is common in Japan – but sounds strange to us!

SAKURA – CHERRY BLOSSOMS

(sah–koo–rah, sah–koo–rah)
SA–KU–RA SA–KU–RA

(sah–koo–rah sah–koo–rah
SAKURA SAKURA
Cherry blossoms! cherry blossoms

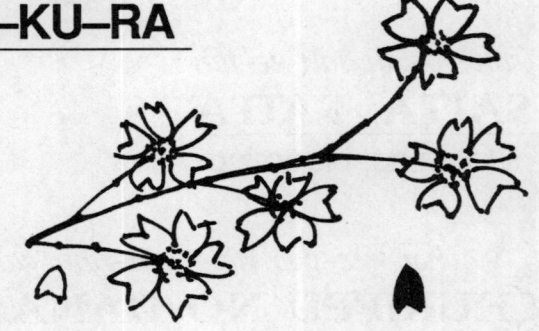

yah–yoh–ee noh soh–rah wah, nee–oh–ee zoh ee–zoo–rah
YAYOI NO SORA WA, NIOI ZO IZURA
March skies   smell of cherry blossoms

ee–zah–yah, ee–zah–yah, mee–nee yoo–kahn)
I ZA YA, I ZA YA, MINI YUKAN.
Let's go! and see the blossoms.

Remember – oo is like "zoo"

This is a "FINGER" SONG
MUSUNDE HIRAITE

MUSUNDE, HIRAITE
TE O UTE, MUSUNDE,
MATA HIRAI TE, TE O UTE,
SONO TE O UE NI...

This is how you sing it... and move your hands.

(moo–oo–oo soo–oon deh hee–rah ee–ee–teh
MU – U – SU – UN –DE HI – RA – I T E
make a fist   open your hand

teh–oh–ho oo–teh   *moo–oo–soo–oon deh*
TE O – O U – TE   MU – U– SU – UNDE
clap hands   make a fist

mah–tah –hee–rah–ee –teh   *teh oh oo–oo teh*
MA – TA HI–RAI –TE   TE O UTE
again – open your hands   clap your hands

soh–noh–oh–teh–oh .... oo–eh nee)
SO – NO TE O U – E NI
then put your hands up high over your head.

TONGUE TWISTERS

1. *(nah–mah–moo–gee)*
   NAMA MUGI!

   (nah–mah–goh–meh)
   NAMA GOME!

   (nah–mah–tah–mah–goh)
   NAMA TAMAGO!

   It means: Raw grain, raw rice, raw eggs!

(nah–mah) **NAMA** RAW		*(kah–kee)* **KAKI** PERSIMMON	
(moo–gee) **MUGI** GRAIN		*(bōh–zoo)* **BOZU** PRIEST	
(goh–meh) **GOME** RICE		*(byō–boo)* **BYŌBU** SCREEN	
(ta–mago) **TAMAGO** EGGS		*(jōh–zoo)* **JOZU** TO DO WELL	
(toh–nah–ree) **TONARI** NEIGHBOR		*(eh)* **E** PAINTING	
(kya–koo) **KYAKU** GUEST		*(kah–ee–tah)* **KAITA** TO WRITE	

2. *(Toh–nah–ree noh kyah–koo wah yoh–koo kah–kee koo kyah–koo dah!)*
   TONARI NO KYAKU WA YOKU KAKI KU KYAKU DA!
   And it means: The guest next door eats a lot of persimmons!

3. *(Bōh–zoo gah byō–boo nee jōh–zoo nah bōh–zoo noh eh oh kah–ee–tah!)*
   BŌZU GA BYŌBU NI JŌZU NA BŌZU NO E O KAITA!
   And it means: The priest skillfully drew a priest's picture on the screen.

(oh–ree–gah–mee)
ORIGAMI
PAPER FOLDING

Japanese children love to make things by folding **SQUARE** pieces of colored or patterned paper. This is called **ORIGAMI. KAMI** *(kah–mee)* is the Japanese word for paper. Children, even in kindergarten, learn to make simple things out of paper. If you don't have any Japanese **ORIGAMI** paper, don't worry! Last years' Christmas paper, gift wrappings, even colored ad pages from magazines make beautiful **ORIGAMI**. It is very important that you start out with a perfect square. Then fold the paper carefully and accurately, following directions on the next few pages. Start with a square 8" x 8", and about the same weight as this page.

Surprise your friends!

The Tongue Cut Sparrow! (page 101)

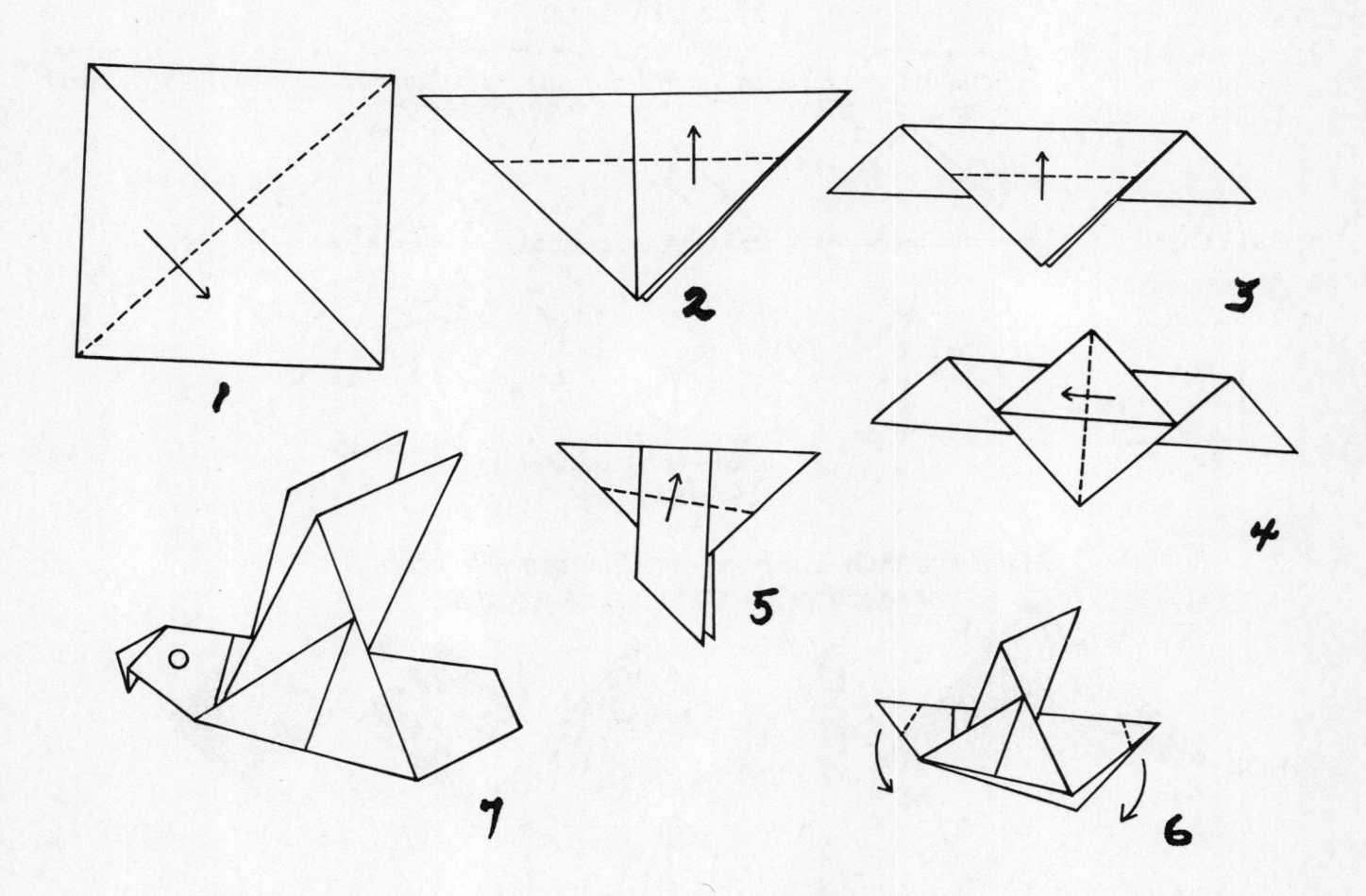

ORIGAMI
PAPER FOLDING

(kah–boo–toh)
KABUTO
SAMURAI HELMET . . . a "helmet"

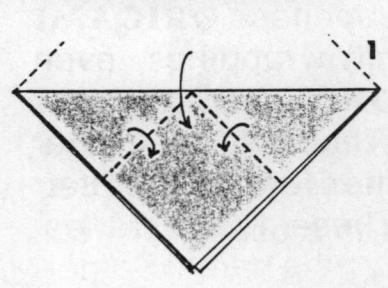

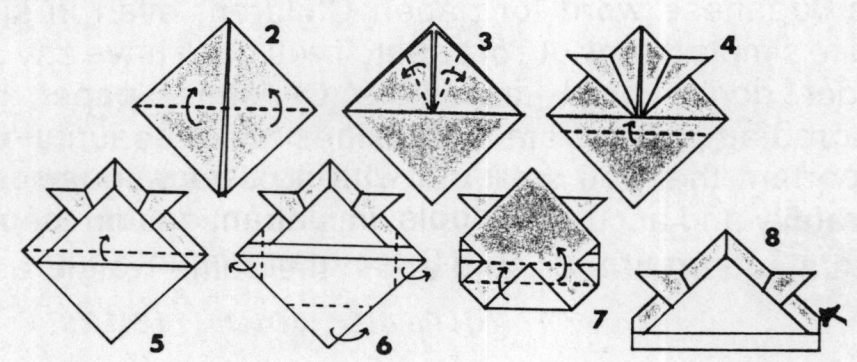

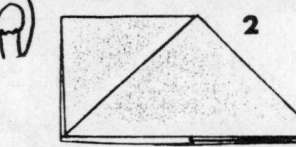

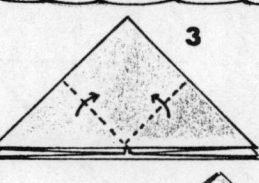

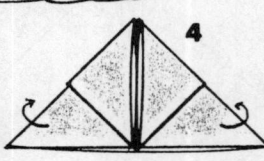

SAMURAI HELMET

(foo–sehn)
FUSEN
A balloon
(Remember to blow in the little hole in the bottom)

BALLOON

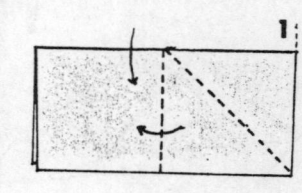

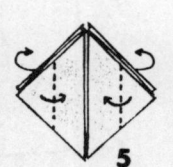

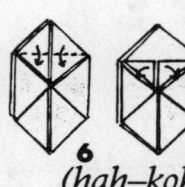

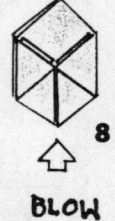

(hah–koh)
HAKO
A box
Make your own little boxes, and fill them with peanuts or candy for your next birthday party!

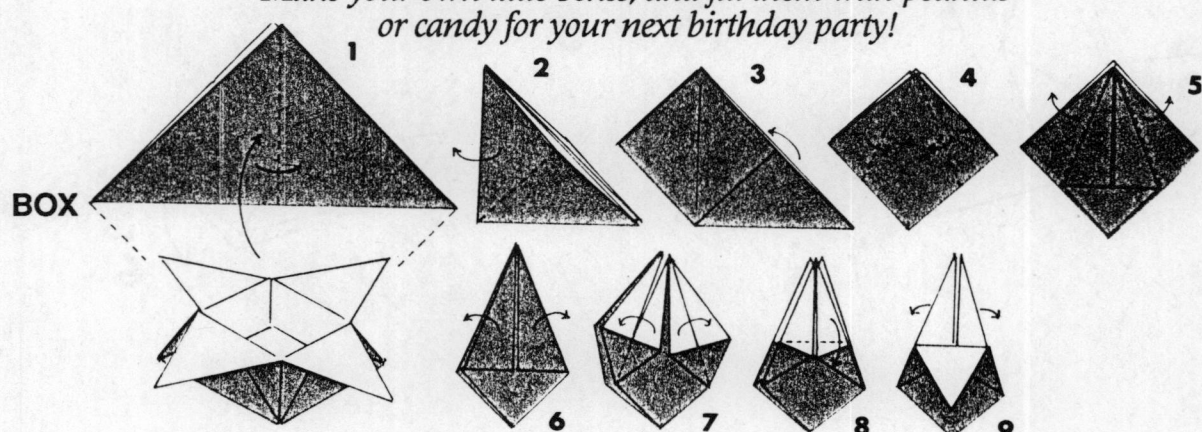

BOX

116

CRANE

千 SEN

羽 BA

鶴 ZURU or TSURU

(sehn–bah tsoo–roo)
**SENBA TSURU
1,000 CRANES**

Sometimes friends and relatives fold 1,000 colorful, paper cranes for *"get–well"* or *"good–luck"* wishes. During baseball competition between high schools in Japan, students often make **SENBA ZURU** for their school team. These 1,000 cranes are hung right in the dugout during the game! Sometimes **SENBA TSURU** are given to patients in the hospital. **"Get well soon."**

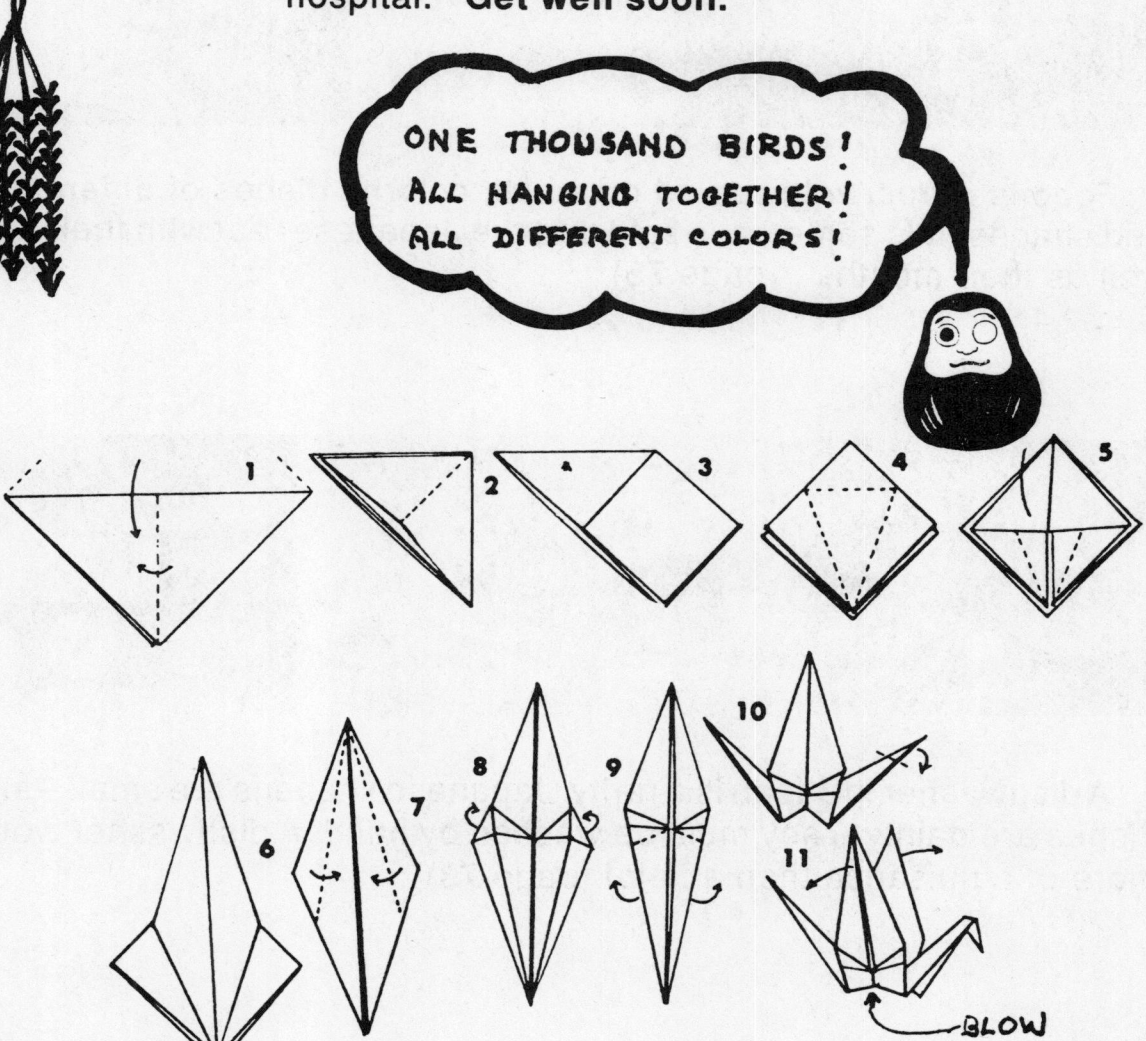

*ONE THOUSAND BIRDS!
ALL HANGING TOGETHER!
ALL DIFFERENT COLORS!*

BLOW

117

The capital of Japan, Tokyo. On one side of the moat is the Imperial Palace – on the otherside are modern skyscrapers. (page 130)

Food is attractively served on small, colorful dishes of different sizes and shapes. It is sometimes said that the Japanese "eat with their eyes as well as their mouths". (page 75)

A dishwasher in Japan is a rarity. Japanese kitchens are small – and the dishes are dainty. They must be washed by hand. A dishwasher would be more of a nuisance than a help! (page 73)

(Photos courtesy of Japan National Tourist Organization.)

Chapter 10

This and That

JAPANESE MONEY . . . PAPER

JAPANESE MONEY . . . COINS

HOW MUCH IS IT?

LETTER . . . ENVELOPES . . . STAMPS

ANIMAL TALK

JANKENPON . . . THREE MONKEYS

MOSHI MOSHI . . . **MOCHI** . . . **MUSHI**

PUSSY WILLOWS

CHOPSTICKS AND **HASHI OKI**

MAP OF JAPAN

EMPEROR OF JAPAN

FLAG OF JAPAN

KAO – **KANJI** for face

OWARI – THE END!

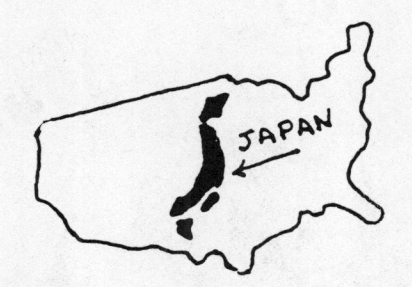

あ AH
れ RE
こ KO
れ RE

THAT

THIS

(ah–reh koh–reh)
ARE KORE

(nee pohn noh o kah neh)
NIPPON NO OKANE
JAPANESE MONEY

(oh sah tsoo)
OSATSU
Japanese paper money

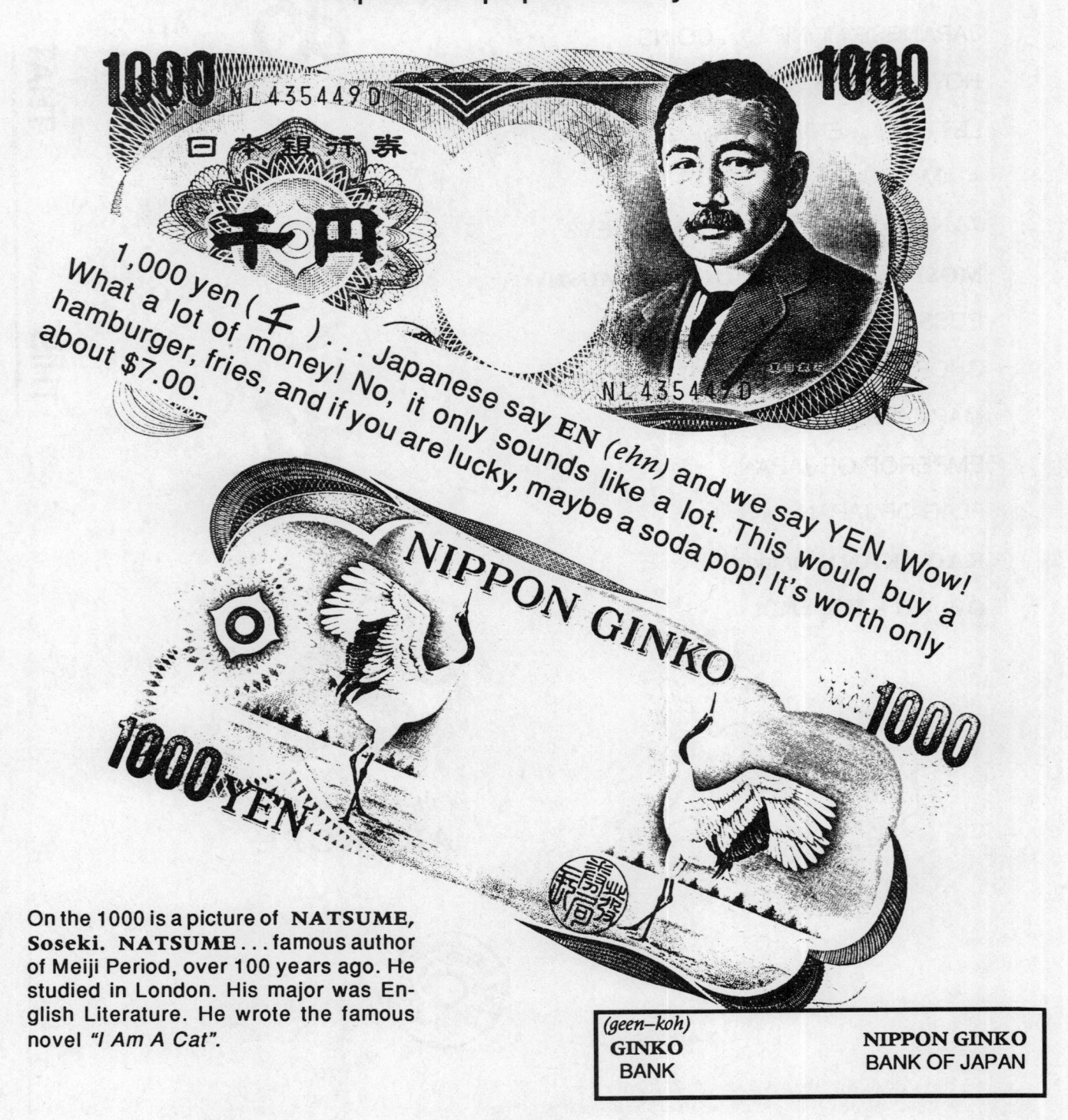

¥ *is the sign for YEN*

1,000 yen (千) . . . Japanese say EN *(ehn)* and we say YEN. Wow! What a lot of money! No, it only sounds like a lot. This would buy a hamburger, fries, and if you are lucky, maybe a soda pop! It's worth only about $7.00.

On the 1000 is a picture of **NATSUME, Soseki. NATSUME** . . . famous author of Meiji Period, over 100 years ago. He studied in London. His major was English Literature. He wrote the famous novel *"I Am A Cat"*.

(geen–koh)
GINKO
BANK

NIPPON GINKO
BANK OF JAPAN

120

OSATSU

If you look closely you can see a blank area on the paper money – **OSATSU**. Only when you hold it up to the light can you see a man's face in the space . . . almost like magic! It is the face of the same man whose picture you see on the **OSATSU**. This is a reduced size The actual size of the **OSATSU** is on the preceding page.

OSATSU for 5000 yen (1992) worth about $35.21

NITOBE, Inazo: well known Christian educator during **Meiji** Period, over 100 years ago. Helped introduce Christianity to Japan. Principal of the First High School(**DAI ICHI**) now the famous Tokyo University . . . #1 in Japan.

Japanese Paper Money

1,000 **ISSEN** EN
5,000 **GOSEN** EN
10,000 **ICHI MAN** EN

FUKUZAWA, Yukichi: educator and economist. One of the first Japanese to visit the US after Japan was opened to "the west" in the late 1800's. Founder of famous old **Keio** University . . . still an "Ivy League" school!

There is also a ¥500 OSATSU

Japanese Periods

Keio . . . . – 1868
Meiji . . . . 1868 – 1912
Taisho . . . 1912 – 1928
Showa . . . 1928 – 1989
Heisei . . . .1989 –

121

JAPANESE OKANE cont'

(kōh kah)
KŌKA
COINS

¥ = 円

KANJI FOR YEN

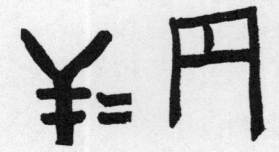

The smallest coin is 1¥
The largest coin is 500¥

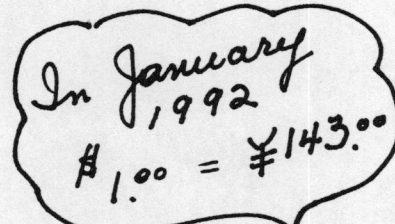

In January 1992 $1.00 = ¥143.00

The following values are approximate – the ratio changes daily.

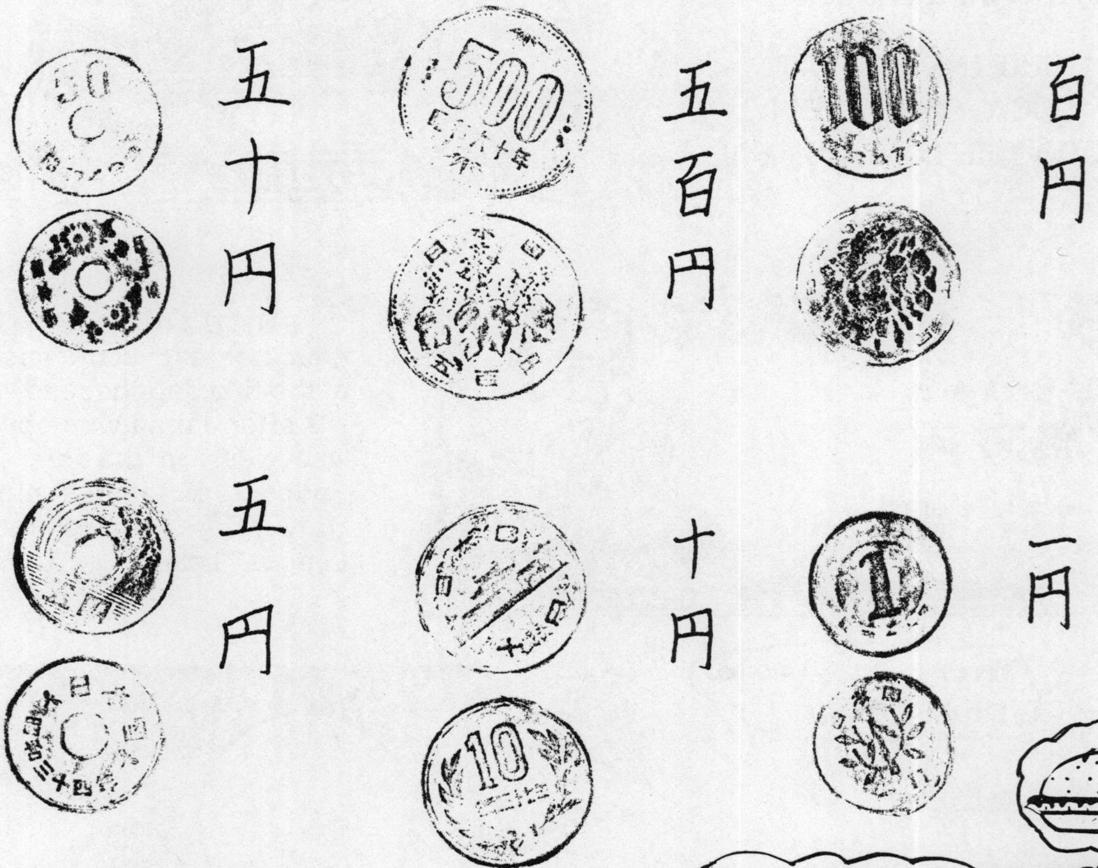

五十円 — 50

五百円 — 500

百円 — 100

五円 — 5

十円 — 10

一円 — 1

Wow! 500¥ for a hamburger.

The Japanese say 'en' – we say 'yen'!

122

(ee–koo–rah dehss kah?)
IKURA DESU KA?
How much does it cost?

(tah–kah–ee)
TAKAI
expensive

(yah–soo–ee)
YASUI
cheap

(ree–n–goh wah ee–koo–rah deh–ss kah?)
RINGO WA IKURA DESU KA?
How much are the apples or how much is the apple?

(yah–soo–ee dehss neh)
YASUI DESU NE?
Cheap, aren't they or cheap, isn't it?

(sahn joo goh ehn deh–ss)
SAN JŪ GO EN DESU.
Thirty five yen.

Singular and plural are the same in Japanese

(mahn)
1 MAN = 10,000

(jee–tehn–shah wah ee–koo–rah dehss kah)
JITENSHA WA IKURA DESU KA?
How much is the bike?

ICHI MAN YON SEN KYU HYAKU EN DESU.
Fourteen thousand nine hundred yen.

(teh–gah–mee)　　(foo–toh)　　(keet–teh)
TEGAMI – FŪTŌ – KITTE
LETTER – ENVELOPE – STAMP

Japanese **KITTE** *are beautiful*
1992 postage U.S. ⟶ Japan = 50¢
Japan ⟶ U.S. =   100 (69¢)

DO YOU NOTICE ANYTHING PECULIAR ABOUT THIS FŪTŌ

a FŪTŌ is an envelope

The return address is written on the back of **FŪTŌ**. *The envelope is addressed "backwards" to our way of writing in U.S.!*

124

HOW DO ANIMALS TALK?

Do animals in Japan speak Japanese?

US		JAPAN
MEOW! MEOW! cat	(neh–koh) **NEKO**	(nee–ah–oo, nee–ah–oo) **NIAU, NIAU**
BOW WOW! dog	(ee–noo) **INU**	(wahn wahn) **WAN-WAN, WAN-WAN**
OINK! OINK! pig	(boo–tah) **BUTA**	(boo–boo, boo–boo) **BUU-BUU, BUU-BUU**
MOO-MOO! cow	(oo–shee) **USHI**	(moh–moh, moh–moh) **MOH-MOH MOH-MOH**
HEEEEEE! horse	(oo–mah) **UMA**	(hee–heen, hee–heen) **HI-HIN, HI-HIN**
BAA-BAA! sheep	(hee–tsoo–jee) **HITSUJI**	(mehhhhh, mehhhh) **MEEEEEEEE**
COCK–A–DOODLE–DO rooster	(nee–wah–toh–ree) **NIWATORI**	(koh–keh–kohk–koh! koh–keh–kohk–koh!) **KO–KE–KOKKO**

Can animals in Japan understand animals in US?
Yes, I think they understand each other. Don't you?

(jahn–kehn–pohn)
JANKENPON

Americans sometimes spin a coin to decide *"who goes first"*! What do the Japanese do? They play **JAN KEN PON**. Children especially, love to play this game. Someone shouts **"jankenpo"**, and at the same time the players form shapes with their hands. A fist means stone and two outstretched fingers indicate scissors, and an open hand means paper. If one person makes a fist (stone) and the other person shows an open hand (paper), who is the winner? Paper, of course . . . as paper wraps stone. Paper wraps stone, but scissors cut paper, and a stone can break scissors!

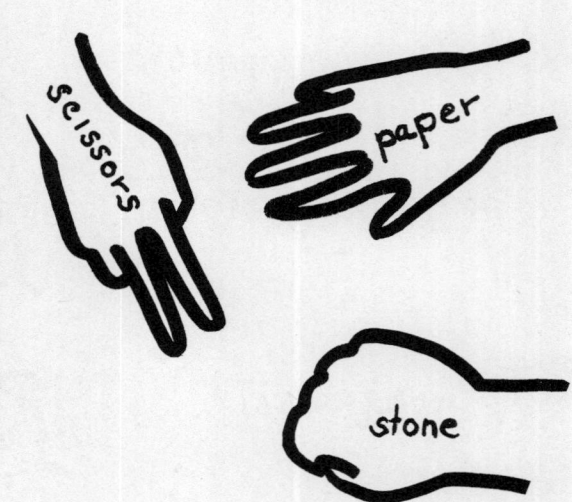

SEE NO EVIL . . . SPEAK NO EVIL . . . HEAR NO EVIL

In the famous, old city of **NIKKŌ** there are many beautiful temples, pagodas, and bridges. Above the entrance of one ancient shrine is a carved, wooden panel of three monkeys. What do they look like they are doing? Can you guess? The one covering his eyes is saying *"SEE NO EVIL"*. One is saying *"HEAR NO EVIL"*. The third one is covering his mouth. What is he trying to tell you? These monkeys are famous throughout the world.

Can you find Nikko on the map of Japan? (page 129)

MOSHI–MOSHI . . . MUSHI . . . MOCHI . . .

Don't confuse these words . . . They sound very much alike, don't they?

(moh–shee moh–shee)
MOSHI–MOSHI
This is what the Japanese always say when they start to talk on the telephone! "HELLO! HELLO! Are you there?" **MOSHI! MOSHI!** (page 19)

(moo–shee)
MUSHI
This is the Japanese word for worm, or bug!

(moh–chee)
MOCHI
This is the special cake made out of sweet rice! (page 84)

So . . . when you pick up the phone please say **"MOSHI-MOSHI"** . . . not "mushi-mushi", or "mochi-mochi"!

PUSSY WILLOWS
(neh–koh yah–nah–gee)
and NEKO YANAGI

In Japanese a **NEKO** is a *"cat"* . . . or *"pussy"*, and a **YANAGI** is a *"willow"* tree. Did we copy the Japanese . . . or did they copy us? Who really gave the soft, grey PUSSY WILLOW its name? These trees are found in both countries!

(hah–shee)
HASHI
CHOPSTICKS

In Japan **HASHI** are used for eating, instead of a knife, fork and spoon. They are usually made of wood, but sometimes of plastic. Restaurants use disposable **HASHI**. Sometimes they are called **OHASHI**. Adults usually say **'OHASHI'**.

(hah–shee oh–kee)
HASHI OKI

HASHI OKI are little chopstick *'rests'*, used in special restaurants or for guests. They are made of wood, plastic or china, and come in different shapes . . maybe a fish, a flower, a cat, a leaf, etc.

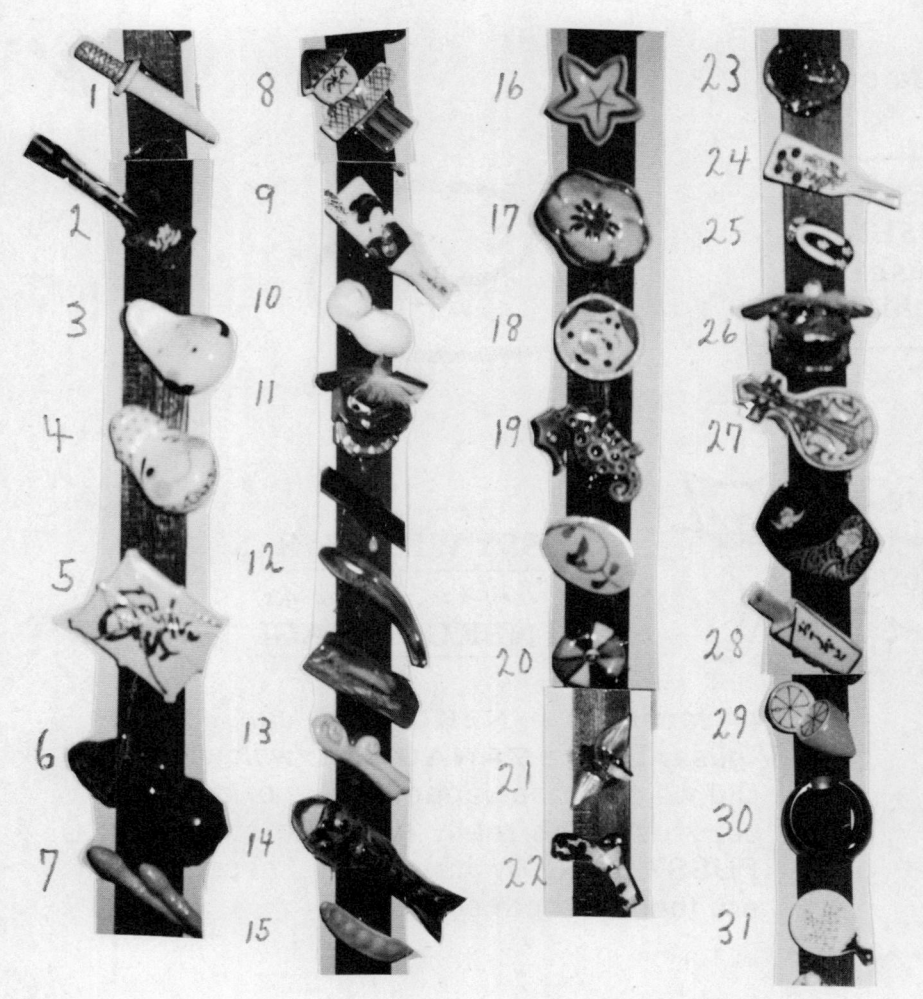

Can you guess what these HASHI OKI are?

1. sword, 2. **SAMISEN** – musical instrument, 3. woman's face mask, 4. man's face mask, 5. kite, 6. dog, 7. *'horse tail'* – gathered in the springtime and eaten, 8. **HE NO HE NO MO HE JI** face boy (page 61), 9. **HAGOITA** battledore, 10. cat, 11. devil's mask, 12. fish, 13. fern frond . . . gathered in the springtime and eaten, 14. fish, 15. pea pod, 16. maple leaf, 17. flower, 18. face, 19. sea horse, 20. ball, 21. **TSURU** crane, 22. bow, 23. chestnut, 24. **HAGOITA**, 25. **ZORI** foot wear similar to **GETA**, 26. **ONI** devil's mask, 27. musical instrument, 28. **HASHI** in case, 29. lemon and slice, 30. ring, 31. fan.

128

JAPAN'S FOUR MAIN ISLANDS

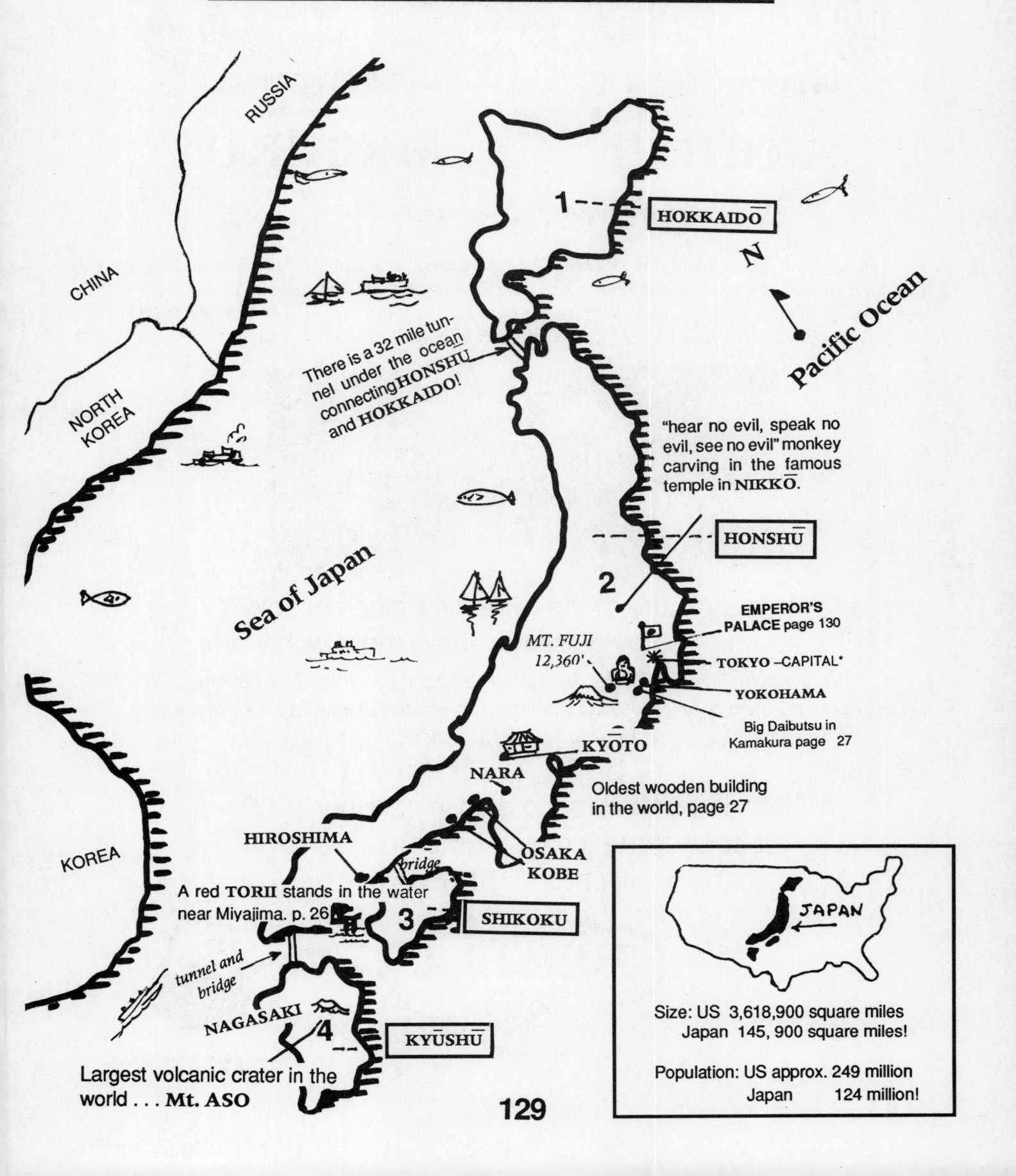

RUSSIA

CHINA

NORTH KOREA

KOREA

Sea of Japan

Pacific Ocean

N

1 — HOKKAIDŌ

There is a 32 mile tunnel under the ocean connecting HONSHU and HOKKAIDO!

"hear no evil, speak no evil, see no evil" monkey carving in the famous temple in NIKKŌ.

2 — HONSHŪ

MT. FUJI 12,360'

EMPEROR'S PALACE page 130
TOKYO – CAPITAL*
YOKOHAMA
Big Daibutsu in Kamakura page 27

KYOTO
NARA

Oldest wooden building in the world, page 27

HIROSHIMA
bridge
OSAKA
KOBE

3 — SHIKOKU

A red TORII stands in the water near Miyajima. p. 26

tunnel and bridge

NAGASAKI

4 — KYŪSHŪ

Largest volcanic crater in the world... Mt. ASO

JAPAN

Size: US 3,618,900 square miles
Japan 145,900 square miles!

Population: US approx. 249 million
Japan 124 million!

JAPAN IS NOW A DEMOCRACY
(since World War II)

but it also has...

AN EMPEROR NAMED
(ah–kee–hee–toh)
AKIHITO

and

AN EMPRESS NAMED
(mee–chee–koh)
MICHIKO

Japan's first emperor was in 660 B.C.

*He is now just a figure-head like the kings and queens of England. But for decades before, and during World War II (until September 1945), Japanese soldiers wanted to die for their Emperor. When they couldn't be victorious in battle they committed suicide (**HARAKIRI**) for their Emperor Hirohito, rather than return to Japan alive and in disgrace.*

This is a picture of the Imperial Palace in Tokyo.
It is surrounded by gardens, and a moat with water.

The Emperor is not elected by the people – his reign goes from father to son. The Japanese system of government is similar to the British system. They both elect prime ministers. We elect a president.

(hee–roh–hee–toh)
When Emperor Hirohito died in January 1989 – Akihito became the new Emperor. His reign is called **HEISEI**.

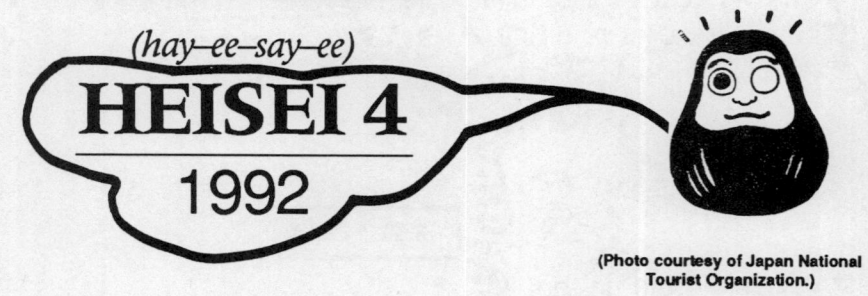

(hay–ee–say–ee)
HEISEI 4
1992

(Photo courtesy of Japan National Tourist Organization.)

130

(neep–pohn)   (nee–hohn)
NIPPON or NIHON
JAPAN

When you see the word **NIPPON** or **NIHON** it means Japan.

A **NIHON JIN** is a Japanese person.

NI – **KANJI** for day, daytime, sunshine and **SUN**

HON (PON) – **KANJI** for book, natural, proper and **ORIGIN**

HINOMARU
Japanese Flag

(hee noh mah–roo)
HI NO MARU

"Maru" means "round"

"Hi" means "sun"

a red ball on a white background.

Japan is known as the "land of the rising sun".

KANJI FOR "FACE"

Can you learn these parts of "KAO".

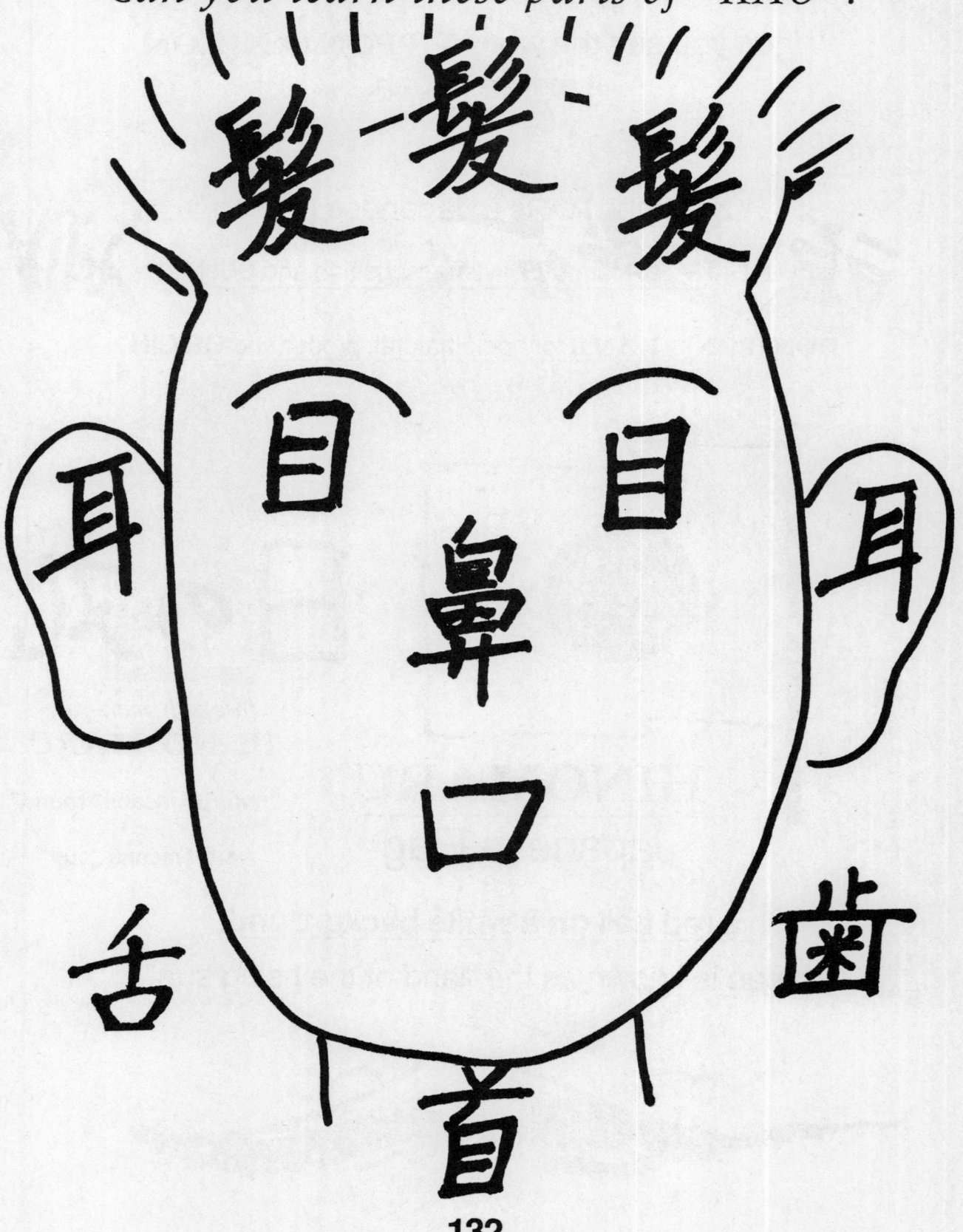

髪　髪　髪
耳　目　目　耳
鼻
口
舌　　　歯
首

Always follow stroke numbers.

(ah–tah–mah)
ATAMA
HEAD

"Wow! It's so much easier to just write head."

(hah)
HA
TEETH

(mee–mee)
MIMI
EAR

(meh)
ME
EYE

目

(koo–chee)
KUCHI
MOUTH

口

(shee–tah)
SHITA
TONGUE

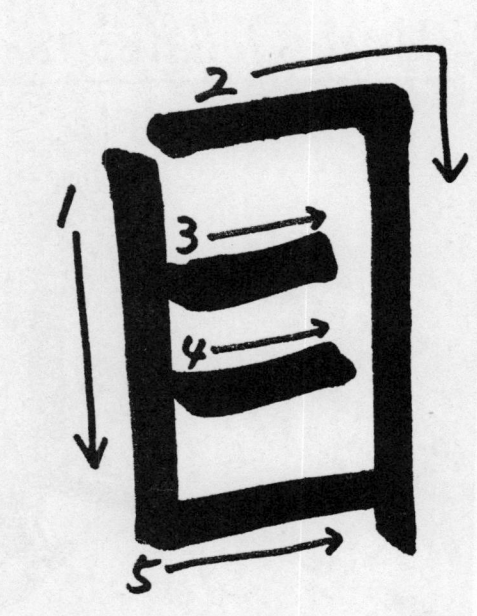

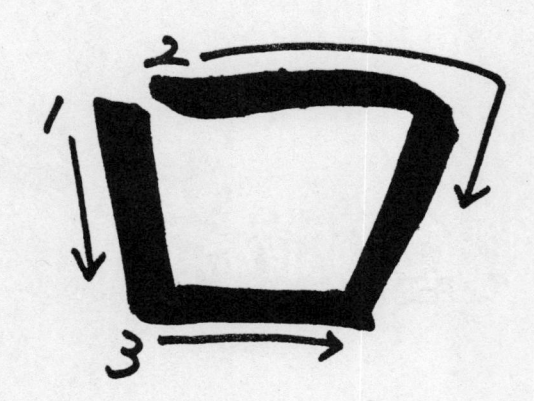

舌

(hah–nah)
HANA
NOSE

鼻

(koo–bee)
KUBI
NECK

首

(kah–mee)
KAMI
HAIR

髪

NOW YOU CAN KANJI YOUR OWN FACE!

鼻
首
髪

When you can write these KANJI – you have 'graduated' from this book!

(oh–wah–ree)
OWARI

THE END

FLORENCE E. METCALF
© 1992
15805 SE 12th Pl.
Bellevue, Washington 98008
(206) 746-2853